Virtualization Changes Everything:
Storage Strategies for
VMware vSphere & Cloud Computing
by Vaughn Stewart & Michael Slisinger

Cover Image: © Vaughn Stewart
Cover Design: Vaughn Stewart

Trademarks
Many of the designations used by manufacturers and sellers to distinguish their products are claimed as Trademarks. Trademark names may appear in this book. Rather than use a trademark symbol with every occurrence of the trademarked name, the authors use the names only in an editorial fashion and to the benefit of the trademark owner, with no intention of infringement of the trademark. No such use, or the use of any trade name, is intended to convey endorsement or other affiliation with this book.

The example companies, organization, products, domain names, e-mail addresses, logos, people, places and events depicted herein are fictitious. No association with any real company, organization, product, domain name, e-mail address, logo, person, place, or event is intended or should be inferred.

Notice of Liability
This book expresses the authors' views and opinions. The information contained in this book is provided without any express, statutory, or implied warranties.

ISBN: 978-1479112562
LCCN:
Printed and bound in the United States of America

Table of Contents

Acknowledgments

The authors would like to acknowledge the following individuals for their contributions and/or assistance:

Scott Baker
Friea Berg
Frank Denneman
Duncan Epping
Gary Hocking
Dr. Stephen Herrod
Larry Touchette

To Mike & Tiger, for their sharing their talents and extending their patience.

    -Vaughn Stewart

To Mom and Grandma, for showing me the way.

To Elizabeth, for supporting this work, even when I was writing "on her time."

To Michelle, my genetic best friend.

To Lillian, for inspiring me to be better.

    -Michael Slisinger

Foreword

Cloud computing, and the underlying virtual infrastructure it relies on, continues to change the way architects design and deploy physical infrastructure technologies. Many view cloud computing as the means to maximize resource utilization in an agile, flexible, robust and efficient way.

Storage technologies are a core component of any datacenter. Their usage in a cloud architecture is ever-changing. They have requirements that span beyond the traditional storage functionality of availability and performance. The capabilities of virtualization and cloud computing, and advancements in areas of integration, place requirements on today's architects to develop expertise across the entire infrastructure stack.

Building storage virtualization expertise depends on a solid foundation from which decisions and architectures can be constructed. Principles that must be considered include scalability, availability, flexibility, level of integration and, of course, cost. This book reviews these attributes as they specifically apply to supporting a software-driven datacenter.

Vaughn and Mike attempt to share how to better align storage technologies with the demands of a virtual infrastructure. The information, considerations and recommendations contained within this book are necessary to understanding how to design, build and deploy a storage platform capable of delivering benefits in accordance with cloud computing initiatives.

Duncan Epping – Principal Architect, VMware, Inc.

Introduction

Virtualization changes everything – it is the "Swiss Army Knife" of Information Technology (IT) departments around the world: it's the enabler that helps IT departments to save money, keep applications running, and to respond even faster to growing customer demands. What's more, virtualization offers these revolutionary benefits in an evolutionary way, applying them to both existent and new applications and hardware investments. The resulting reach is profound: IDC estimates that as of 2010, more than half of all enterprise workloads were virtualized, with even further acceleration towards virtualization on the horizon.

We have entered a new era of computing and transformation within the IT industry, fueled by the movement away from rigid infrastructure silos to flexible and dynamic shared resource pools: I refer to this model as a "cloud infrastructure." Cloud computing is the ideal medium for businesses to adapt to the dynamic needs of their customers, overcome challenges, and deliver the right solutions at the right time. An effective cloud infrastructure enables businesses to thrive in the face of uncertain demands, and to benefit in ways such as:

Cost Reductions and Economies of Scale: A combination of technologies that delivers resources on-demand in order to optimize utilization, reduce complexity, and more effectively manage workloads and operational tasks.

Business and IT Agility: Deploying resources on-demand enables organizations to take advantage of new opportunities, and to address business conditions on much shorter timescales.

Redefining Hardware Resources: Virtualization creates an opportunity to abstract design considerations and processes from the hardware layers and turn hardware attributes into service level agreements, supporting the on-demand nature of the infrastructure.

The foundation underlying cloud computing is the virtual infrastructure. In order to create a dynamic, software-driven datacenter, one that is elastic and capable of scaling both vertically and horizontally, architects must have an optimized and aligned virtual and physical infrastructure strategy. This strategy enables the mobilization of datacenter resources, and on-demand delivery of those resources in a manner that is workload and service focused.

This strategy is also needed to guide decisions and actions concerning infrastructure investments. These investment decisions are particularly challenging as there are multiple virtualization technologies to choose from, and there are a greater number of architectural layers to consider (servers, network, storage, applications, management, etc.). A successful cloud infrastructure depends on selecting technologies that meet today's business needs, along with inherent flexibility to meet the undefined needs of tomorrow.

These virtualization infrastructure technologies are the focus of this book. The information and considerations contained within are necessary to understand the in-depth requirements for designing, building, and deploying a cloud computing platform capable of delivering the benefits above. Ultimately, this book serves as a guide to craft the infrastructure component of one's virtualization strategy with considerations for virtualization and cloud workloads. Vaughn and Michael draw upon years of practical experience to help you make educated decisions as you develop the virtualization strategy that is your legacy, and that will take your organization to the next stage in your journey to a software-driven datacenter.

Virtualization is the tool that changes everything we do, and everything that we do has a direct effect on virtualization.

Dr. Stephen Herrod – Chief Technology Officer, VMware, Inc.

About the Authors

Vaughn Stewart:

Vaughn is the Director for Cloud Computing Solutions at NetApp, where he assists in setting the strategic direction for cloud-based solutions – a rewarding role that blends his engineering interests with his enthusiasm for engaging clients, vendors, and leaders in the IT industry. He is the virtualization evangelist for NetApp. He shares his thoughts on the role of storage with cloud computing on his blog, http://virtualstorageguy.com. Vaughn is also a frequent presenter at leading technical conferences and has been recognized by VMware as a vExpert since 2009.

Vaughn resides in the San Francisco Bay area, where he enjoys good coffee, live music, leisure travel, spending time with his girlfriend, and sharing laughter with his friends.

Michael Slisinger:

Michael is a Global Cloud Solutions Architect for NetApp, who focuses on working with NetApp's Service Provider Partners to create innovative and profitable Public Cloud IT as a Service (ITaaS) solutions. He has over 15 years of experience in the industry, and has previously held roles in Technical Marketing and Professional Services. He has been with NetApp since 2003.

Michael lives with his lovely wife and daughter in suburban Detroit, Michigan. In his exceedingly rare moments of free time, he can usually be found rummaging through a mountainous pile of half-read books and unopened movies and video games, or possibly on vacation in Orlando, waiting in line for Space Mountain.

Vytautas Malesh:

Vytautas "Tiger" Malesh is the Head Copywriter at Woodbridge Copywriting in Detroit, Michigan (http://woodbridgecopywriting.com). He has been producing technical and professional documentation for the IT, automotive, advertising, and financial industries for ten years. He also serves as a writing consultant, ghostwriter, and editor, and has taught college-level academic, technical and professional writing since 2006.

When not teaching or producing professional copy, Tiger enjoys writing prose fiction, reading Modern literature, painting, and the occasional night out on the town.

Chapter 1
Storage Matters

Storage Matters

The advent of cloud computing is revolutionizing datacenter design, application support, and end-user service. Every vendor in the storage industry is focused on building highly agile, hardware-independent, software-defined datacenters that employ the coordinated execution of resource and service delivery with shared infrastructure resources as a means to reduce operational and capital expenditures while advancing business objectives.

The authors of this book have been actively developing storage solutions to support the emerging capabilities of virtual infrastructures and private clouds for over 6 years. With the advancements in these technologies over the past several years, we have been consistently surprised by the prevalent assumptive views concerning the role of storage technologies in both advancing and limiting the capabilities of a cloud infrastructure: to wit, most of these views could politely be described as indifferent. Architects often apply natural assumptions concerning the storage layer of their cloud designs: as long as the array can support the assigned workload, is highly available, and offers a high-speed form of interconnect, then (according to the prevailing logic) there is nothing else to worry about.

This position is terribly short-sighted. In order to reap the rewards inherent in virtualization and cloud computing, architects and administrators must aggressively seek out the best storage technologies to support their networks and infrastructures. A fine house built on sand is hardly a home, and a virtual datacenter built on "good enough" equipment will fail to meet the exponentially increasing demands of today's organizations.

VMware drove the rapid growth of virtualization, and heads the march towards an elastic, service-focused cloud computing platform. During this time, they have introduced new storage management and consumption models that have outpaced the innovation of many storage vendors and the storage technologies in existing datacenters. Architectural and data access changes have led to challenges in nearly every aspect of the storage infrastructure, including performance, cost, operational manageability and execution. During this phase, one truth emerged: storage had become the hottest topic in data infrastructure, and old assumptions were being overturned overnight.

In the years since we wrote our first VMware-related technical report to support ESX 2.5, we have met hundreds, if not thousands, of technical architects, engineers, and leaders who have all been plagued by the same handful of storage-related issues. Out of these innumerable conversations, we heard, and found ourselves repeating, one mantra-like phrase:

"Virtualization Changes Everything"

And nothing in the infrastructure stack has been so profoundly changed by the cloud technologies that information architects are buying, designing, and deploying, as the storage array.

The Goal of this Book

The technical reference guide is easily the most common form of technology book. What you have in your hands is not that type of book.

Virtualization Changes Everything is designed to survey the effects cloud computing has had on storage platforms and technologies. We seek to address common goals and challenges faced when deploying a cloud architecture in terms of how storage technologies can better serve the unique needs of cloud computing in areas like resource pooling, rapid elasticity and on-demand self-service for the consumer. We will attempt to guide datacenter architects by providing a critical review of storage technologies deployed either individually or in combination, and to measure their effectiveness, specifically in supporting shared virtual infrastructures.

The concepts and opinions in this book have been written in accordance with what we call **the 90/10 rule**. This rule, simply stated, requires that any cloud or virtualization initiative should strive to satisfy 90 percent of an organization's storage needs. No architecture will ever satisfy 100% of all use cases, but 90% is attainable in a well-designed and intelligently implemented datacenter. Naturally, this means that 10% of use cases will not be satisfied by the solution you put into place, but these fringe users and usages can be easily managed on a case-by-case basis.

We believe that the reviews, references and recommendations that follow will provide solid, vendor-neutral guidance to those responsible for designing cloud architectures, whether from a top-down application or workflow driven perspective, or from an infrastructure, bottom-up view.

For those who seek a greater level of technical detail in areas such as storage connectivity with VMware vSphere, we recommend *Storage Implementation in vSphere 5.0* by Mostafa Khalil, which is available through VMware Press. That book, co-edited by Vaughn Stewart, informs *Virtualization Changes Everything*, and is an excellent technical reference and companion read to this book. Finally, architects and administrators should always seek to review the published best practices from their storage vendor(s). These real-world use cases should help architects deploying a cloud based on VMware vSphere or the virtual infrastructure platforms from Microsoft, Citrix, Red Hat, etc.

Is this Book for You?

If you design or operate a cloud or virtual infrastructure then this book is for you! This is not to say the content in this book wouldn't serve most any storage administrator – it absolutely would! – but we firmly believe that the most significant changes in the datacenter are occurring above the storage layer. Understanding how new and innovative storage technologies can better align with the goals of cloud computing should result in architects being in the best position to meet these goals through the adoption and integration of these advancements.

From a broader perspective, architects need to address the unprecedented global rate of data growth. To be in the best position to tackle the onslaught of "big data," it is a necessity for cloud architects to understand storage technologies and their benefits when deployed in combination. The need for architects to learn and understand this technology is inevitable – for the serious cloud architect, the time is now.

So if your goal is to identify the attributes of a storage platform that are designed to natively support cloud computing with infrastructure capabilities such as dynamic responsiveness to changes in workload, ultra resiliency to failures, and tight integration supporting a software-driven workflow, then this book is for you.

Final Thoughts

A disclaimer: the authors of this book are employed by NetApp. With that being said, know that we are committed to presenting this work in a vendor-neutral manner, and that we apply a critical filter equally to all the technologies we review. Our goal is to promote the adoption of advanced storage technologies regardless of who manufactures them.

Remember that this book is the culmination of years of experience and hundreds of deployments – but it is still only the researched perspective of two virtualization advocates and a diverse cross-section of informal collaborators and correspondents. You may disagree with our findings: that means that you have taken a proactive approach to cloud computing research, and if that enthusiasm is in any way engendered by this book, then we have done our jobs.

What follows are our findings – we share them with you in the interest of promoting this exciting technology. Truly, virtualization changes everything – read on, and see for yourself.

Chapter 2
The Effect of
Virtualization on
Storage

The Effect of Virtualization on Storage

The purpose of *Virtualization Changes Everything* is to review, and provide recommendations regarding, the storage technologies that best meet the needs of a cloud computing platform. Before jumping into business challenges, architectural goals, and an evaluation of technologies, it seems that we should establish how these issues developed over time.

Large-scale technological advancements tend to occur in waves, and are often consumed by customers in an incremental and systematic manner. Such phased approaches can restrict an organization's ability to adopt portions of a technological advancement. Items ranging from the impact that modifying existing processes has on production environments, to timing issues such as software release cycles, are all factors in delayed adoption. We feel the onset of server virtualization and its evolution to cloud computing was just such an event and that during its adoption, many architects and administrators either overlooked or were simply unaware of the effects these technologies were having on the storage array.

With the release of VMware **high availability (HA)**, the adoption of server virtualization moved out of the lab and into the core of the datacenter. HA meant production workloads could now be virtualized with confidence, and the journey to cloud computing began. Coincidentally, along with this explosive growth came the requirement of shared storage, and in turn SAN arrays began requiring upgrades to address subsequent performance and capacity increases. These upgrades resulted in escalating cost increases for the storage infrastructure and subsequent challenges faced in areas such as storage monitoring, capacity management, performance, and backup.

This chapter covers the use of storage by physical servers, and introduces the radical differences in the way virtual infrastructures place requirements on traditional storage platforms. Some may view this chapter as containing basic and well-understood information, but reviewing these fundamental concepts is worthwhile – we hope to explain why hurdles are encountered, and also to track the beginning of trends such as the shift towards NAS, the adoption of storage saving technologies, the emerging preference towards unified Ethernet fabric, and the convergence of backup and disaster recovery processes.

Chapter Sections

This chapter includes the following sections concerning the history of storage and virtualization:

Before Virtualization...Physical Servers
Explains pre-virtualization storage schemes

Virtualization is Born...Meet the Hypervisor
Discusses the creation and increasing prominence of the hypervisor

Storage Reinvented: the Shared Storage Pool
Presents an overview of the relationship between the hypervisor and shared storage resources

The Impact on the Storage Array
Explains some of the challenges present in a shared computing environment

Summary and Recommendations
Acknowledges challenges in shared computing, and transitions into a discussion of solutions

Before Virtualization...Physical Servers

Prior to the advent of server virtualization, the majority of x86-based servers met their data storage requirements through the combined use of **direct attached storage (DAS)** and a local RAID controller. This combination produced a reliable, low-cost form of storage that met the availability requirements for most x86-based workloads. While in wide use, DAS was not viewed by administrators as an ideal means to meet the high performance and resiliency requirements of business-critical applications. For these workloads, datacenters often relied upon SAN, and shortly afterward, NAS arrays.

The traditional shared storage platform is the **SAN array**. SAN arrays, or *SANs*, provided LUNs to hosts via **Fibre Channel**, and over time added additional SCSI based protocols, including **iSCSI** and **Fibre Channel over Ethernet (FCoE)**. As SANs have historically served Fibre Channel, they had significant advantages in storage network bandwidth, and thus were deployed as the means to provide the highest I/O performance for an application.

Note: Some define a SAN as a Fibre Channel-based array. While we understand the arguments for this view, for the purposes of this book, we view a SAN as a shared storage platform that provides SCSI-based LUNs for connectivity via any SCSI-based protocol. FC, iSCSI and FCoE all meet this definition, thus they will all be referred to as SAN. The differences between the use of any one of the three in a virtual infrastructure is miniscule, and similar enough to allow us to group them together for purposes of discussion.

The other choice for a shared storage platform is the **NAS array**. NAS is commonly deployed to allow massive parallel access to filesystems and unstructured datasets by a massive parallel processing server farms and end-users who require access to home directories and department shares. Two of the most common NAS protocols include the **Network File System (NFS)** and **Server Message Block (SMB)** (which was formerly named the **Common Internet File System or CIFS**).

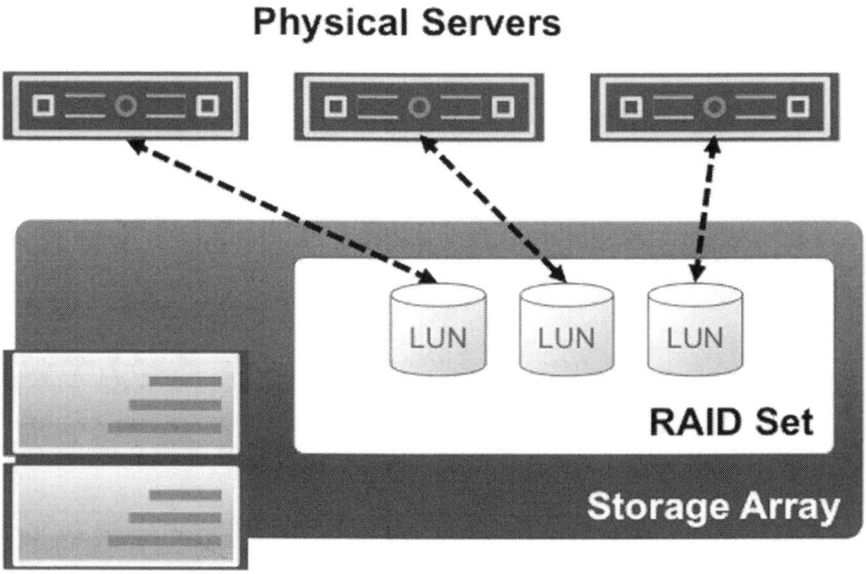

Physical Servers

LUN LUN LUN

RAID Set

Storage Array

Figure 2-1: *An example of a SAN supporting a physical server infrastructure*

When used with physical servers, SAN and NAS arrays provided capabilities that were simply unavailable with DAS, like nonstop data services, high availability for applications, storage of massive volumes of data, fast and efficient hardware-based backups, and the data replication capabilities required for disaster recovery. In addition, both directly map storage resources to servers, which was critical in providing granular resource utilization and consumption on a server-by-server basis.

Virtualization is Born... Meet the Hypervisor

Server virtualization radically changed the many architectural models in the datacenter, ranging from resource consumption to storage provisioning. At the forefront of this technological revolution was the **hypervisor**, which provided the means to change how resources were assigned and consumed by abstracting local server resources and logically representing them as shared resources. These logical resources could be concatenated with the resources of other servers when one or more hypervisors were deployed in a highly available cluster configuration.

Unlike physical servers, hypervisors are designed specifically to be deployed in highly available cluster configurations. This is a very different architecture, one that implements failure domains by requiring data to be served on a shared, highly available storage platform such as a SAN or NAS array. Through this type of fault isolation, the HA mechanism can ensure the restoration of services in the event of a hypervisor failure.

While deploying a cluster is not required, clusters are the norm for datacenter operations due to the enterprise-class features that require shared storage, such as those from VMware like vMotion, DRS, Storage DRS, High Availability, and Fault Tolerance. Shared storage constructs, whether SAN or NAS, support the need to decouple data from physical storage mediums and in turn provide the data mobility required to have a truly dynamic shared virtual infrastructure.

With the introduction of the hypervisor, the old model of assigning physical resources to servers had gone by the wayside – In its place, datacenters gained a new, flexible resource management model enabled by the separation of hardware consumption from physical resources. With the advent of the hypervisor, server virtualization was born.

Storage Reinvented: The Shared Storage Pool

Similar to the aggregation of CPU and memory resources, storage resources are pooled in order to make capacity available to all hosts in a cluster and accessible for on-demand provisioning by VI Administrators. While creating storage pools is not the only means of providing storage to VMs, most hypervisor vendors (and their customers) prefer pools for providing storage in a virtual infrastructure.

Shared storage pools are usually provisioned in a large capacity – exponentially larger than what would be assigned directly to a VM or an individual server. Most virtual machines need storage that appears to be direct-attached in order to operate. This direct attachment can be simulated by the use of **virtual disks**; files presented by the hypervisor to the VM as a virtual hard drive. Virtual disks can be configured as SCSI or ATA devices, but for our conversation this distinction is inconsequential. Shared storage pools do not actually provide storage resources to VMs; instead, they represent the physical resources that store and serve virtual disk files.

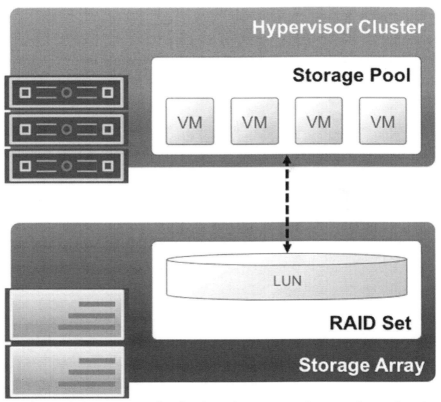

Figure 2-2: *An example of a shared storage pool supporting a virtual infrastructure*

VMware customers are likely to recognize their datastores as being shared storage pools. These and all forms of shared storage pools are often accessed via SAN or NAS protocols, can be comprised of various types of storage media (or drives), and are often used as management boundaries for functions such as data replication, backup or organizational separation.

The shared pool model works well for storage as it enables virtual infrastructure administrators to consume storage resources from the pool without requiring interaction from the storage administration or management teams. Storage pools and virtual disks provide the ability to dynamically provision, clone, and migrate the data of a VM.

The Impact on the Storage Array

When the hypervisor was first introduced, deploying server virtualization with shared storage pools was the only means available to scale an organization's technology infrastructure. As the adoption of server virtualization rapidly grew, the shortcomings of the shared storage pool model became apparent.

The Loss of Data Mapping

With a physical server accessing data from DAS, SAN, or NAS, there was an explicit understanding that the physical storage medium was serving the load of a specific application. Issues related to performance were easy to identify. This capability was lost with SAN-based shared storage pools, and was complicated by the lack of **granular performance information** available when using NAS. This loss of mapping objects to storage resources has driven significant investments by storage and hypervisor vendors to provide better performance management tools.

With direct-attached storage and physical storage devices, an architect or administrator could identify the worthiness of disk drives to meet the load of an application, but the use of shared storage pools resulted in a storage object hosting a number of VMs, and thus being required to serve a significantly larger number of I/O requests. Should one VM become very busy, its disk activity could cause issues for other VMs, or possibly fill storage-side buffers. Storage admins were often unable to identify storage pools operating at peak capacity, and so were unable to identify busy VMs ahead of a performance issue arising.

In addition to these changes, shared storage pools introduced new areas of complexity for storage array-based functions, including snapshot-based backups and restores, granular replication capabilities, performance capability, media type, etc.

An Old Problem Reemerges – Partition Misalignment

For optimal storage and retrieval of data from SCSI devices (such as LUNs), the partition and filesystem which allows a host to access that SCSI device must align its filesystem blocks to the blocks in the storage array. Properly aligned partitions allow efficient data access by the host since at the array level, a request to read a block of data is resolved by retrieving a single block from the disk.

When the partitions of storage devices do not align to the block boundaries of the array, performance will suffer due to **partition misalignment**. This configuration occurs by default when using legacy operating systems, and is prevalent in virtualization deployments. Misaligned partitions result in an increased workload on the array: an I/O request occurring at the host layer will require multiple I/Os by the array since the data will span two or more blocks on the array. This problem can be even worse when writing data, because a request to read a misaligned block would require the array to read two blocks, and the subsequent request to overwrite that block would require the access of four blocks (a read lookup of two blocks followed by a write operation across two blocks).

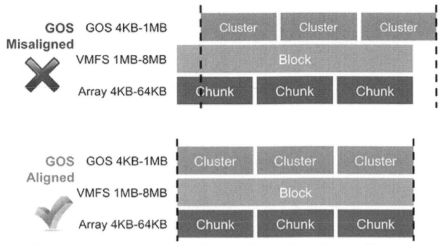

Figure 2-3: *An example of misaligned and aligned guest filesystems*

Storage vendors addressed this issue years ago by providing profiles for LUNs that address the default partition offset found in common operating systems. When formatting a virtual disk, it is treated in the same manner as a physical drive or LUN, and as such the partitions are created without awareness or consideration to the underlying storage array block layout. While this issue was solved with traditional server deployments and LUNs, it has re-emerged with the advent of hypervisors and virtual disks.

This issue is prevalent with VMs running Windows and Linux GOS. Fortunately, modern versions of these operating systems now support a default starting partition offset of 1MB, which universally avoids alignment issues with all forms of storage, from local disks to array platforms.

For those with misaligned partitions in their VMs, I/O performance will suffer by as much as 30%. The increased workload on the storage array can cause significant performance issues and can require additional hardware to be deployed to compensate for the misalignment.

Note: arrays that store data in 512KB sized blocks do not suffer from partition misalignment.

A New Workload and a New Set of Risks

Server virtualization was initially ideal for consolidating under-utilized server resources. The technology and management tools provided by hypervisor vendors helped customers to successfully complete their consolidation goals.

Consolidation meant that these shared storage arrays were now serving very different types of applications. Previously these storage platforms hosted only the most critical applications, after the onset of virtualization they were being used for consolidation. As the applications addressed in a consolidation were often deemed non-critical to business operations, most shared storage pools were deployed with the same RAID data protection technology as an individual physical server.

The use of the shared storage pool meant a storage failure would result in the mass loss of VMs. The outage was equal to the number of VMs stored in the pool. Such a loss could be catastrophic, even when it involved non-critical VMs.

Worse still, many backup solutions were soon identified as less-than-ideal in addressing a mass outage: while the restore of an individual VM could take a few hours, the performance of these traditional backup applications was inadequate for the scale of these failures. The simultaneous loss of multiple VMs compounded the initial failure, and stretched the hours required for service restoration into days.

Increased Storage Costs

Migrating servers, which stored their data on DAS, to VMs storing their data on shared storage arrays resulted in a significant increase in cost to serve the same dataset. While storage has never been identified as a highly-utilized datacenter resource, the shared pool storage model introduced new layers of consumption, which in turn often resulted in decreased storage utilization.

Challenges with Scaling

With mass consolidation, the SCSI-based storage architecture of a SAN was asked to behave differently than in a traditional server environment. Technologies like clustered filesystems were great enablers for virtualization, but they also introduced some unexpected byproducts relating to a number of SCSI-based storage constructs, including LUN-based I/O queues and locking/reservation mechanisms.

Some of these challenges were most pronounced in non-critical operations of scale, such as attempts to complete backup operations in which the backup software required a full backup to be completed on a recurring schedule, or in an unpredicted, dramatic increase in storage costs.

Summary and Recommendations

This chapter may read as though everything at the intersection of storage and server virtualization technologies is chaos and confusion, but not quite – a number of technologies and practices have done much to combat these issues. However, without identifying some of the less desirable byproducts storage systems faced in supporting a shared virtual infrastructure by name, we would be hard-pressed to recommend any method for optimal deployment of a storage infrastructure that provides similar capabilities and benefits as those provided by the higher-level technologies which comprise the cloud, and which avoids the pitfalls of previous iterations of these technologies.

As we move through the following chapters, we will tackle a number of storage technologies applied in cloud computing in greater detail. We will discuss the emergence of Virtual Storage Arrays, storage choices with geo-stretched clusters, and many technologies in between. We will start with one of the most important, contentious, and rapidly changing, aspects of data storage management: the decision to deploy using SAN or NAS.

Chapter 3
SAN & NAS: Storage Protocols in the Cloud

SAN & NAS: Storage Protocols in the Cloud

A key construct in the enablement of cloud computing is the capability of the virtual infrastructure to pool physical datacenter resources in order to be dynamically assigned to any virtual machine within a cluster. Storage is a major component within the cloud, and while the encapsulation of data into files provides the abstraction of the data from the physical disk, it is storage mechanisms that enable the physical storage arrays to support the simultaneous, concurrent access required by a cluster of hypervisors.

Historically, Fibre Channel and Ethernet-based Storage Area Networks (SAN) have been deployed to service the needs of virtual infrastructures. However, over the last 6 years NAS has emerged as a preferred means of storage connectivity for many architects. There are a number of reasons why both SAN and NAS are logical choices for these environments.

The goal of this chapter is to use concrete data points to improve your understanding of deploying SAN and NAS arrays to provide shared data access, including data encapsulation, mobility, manageability, performance, and scale when deploying a shared storage pool. We will discuss the SAN technologies of Fibre Channel, iSCSI, Fibre Channel over Ethernet and the NAS technologies of the **Network File System (NFS)** and the **Server Message Block (SMB)**.

Chapter Sections

This chapter includes the following sections as they relate to deploying shared pool of storage with SAN and NAS connectivity.

Storage Choices
An introduction to SAN, NAS and Guest-connected storage options

Shared Storage Pools
Reviews in-depth the pros and cons of the primary means of providing storage to a virtual infrastructure

Storage Network Fabrics
A summary of network fabric considerations related to SAN and NAS protocols

Storage Performance
Covers storage issues that may potentially cause I/O bottlenecks and limit optimal performance

Storage Management of a Shared Storage Pool
Reviews the capabilities native to the cloud and storage administrative teams

Storage Integration with a Shared Storage Pool
Summarizes the level of storage integration available to cloud-based functions

Summary and Recommendations
Summarizes the strengths and challenges of SAN and NAS-based shared pools

Storage Choices

Whether it is deployed on SAN or NAS, the shared storage pool is the standard means for providing physical storage resources to support a virtual infrastructure. This is because the globally accepted method of providing storage resources to virtual machines is in the form of connecting virtual SCSI disks to virtual machines. In order to take advantage of the advanced capabilities of modern hypervisor platforms, these virtual disk files are required to be stored in a shared storage pool, like a VMware datastore. Common forms of virtual disks files include the Virtual Machine Disk Format from **VMware (VMDK)** and the **Virtual Hard Disk (VHD)** from Microsoft.

Most hypervisors support a wide range of storage connectivity options, and there is a case to be made for all of them.

The Case for Deploying Storage Area Networks

From a historical perspective, SANs have been considered to be the ideal storage platform for hosting mission-critical applications. With this understanding, it is reasonable to suggest that when most customers began to deploy virtual infrastructures, SAN platforms were viewed as the logical choice in storage technology, leading to their prevalence in storage connectivity today.

SAN storage arrays are available from almost every storage vendor, including Dell, EMC, HP, IBM, NetApp, and startups like Nimble Storage. Each vendor offers a common set of core capabilities, as well as unique set of features, functionality, and hypervisor integration.

The Case for Deploying Network Attached Storage

NAS storage arrays have historically been the storage platform of choice when provisioning storage resources for applications requiring massive parallel I/O operations and supporting end user data. The most recognized uses of NAS include user data stored in home directories and department shares, and high performance computational and rendering farms. These types of architectures are often comprised of hundreds or thousands of compute nodes requiring access to a common set of data in order to complete their processing.

NAS storage arrays are available from a number of vendors, including Dell, EMC, HP, IBM, NetApp and startups like Tintri. Each vendor offers a common set of core capabilities, as well as unique sets of features, functionality and hypervisor integration.

Guest Connected Storage – Mapping Storage Directly to VMs

There are a number of application configurations that either require, or are best served, when storage resources are directly connected to the virtual machine. For some applications, accessing a virtual disk residing on a shared storage pool is not an option. This method of storage connectivity is generically referred to as **Guest Connected Storage (GCS)**. While GCS can operate with SAN and NAS protocols, it is currently not suited as a viable replacement for shared storage pools. We will cover this form of connectivity in depth in Chapter 4, Guest Connected Storage.

Shared Storage Pools

SAN-Based Shared Storage Pools

SAN is a logical choice to provide storage services, as it is well understood and trusted as a platform to support the most demanding workloads. SANs can function over Fibre Channel and Ethernet networks. Natively, a SAN is incapable of providing simultaneous data access to multiple hosts. In order to provide the functionality of a shared storage pool, a SAN must be managed by a clustered filesystem, like VMware's **VMFS** or Microsoft's **NTFS Cluster Shared Volumes**.

At a high level, clustered filesystems implement mechanisms that govern the read and write access of a LUN. They often provide simultaneous read access, and broker the ability to write to an individual host, which can write data usually to a reserved range of blocks on the LUN. The brokering model creates a shared mechanism in which all hosts can complete their write operations without interfering with the operations and data integrity of the other hosts.

Below is an image of a shared pool of SAN storage being presented to a cluster of hypervisors:

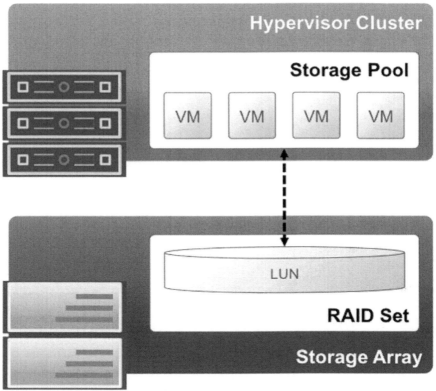

Figure 3-1: *An example of shared SAN storage pool being accessed by a hypervisor cluster*

NAS-Based Shared Storage Pools

NAS platforms are natively designed to provide multiple hosts simultaneous data access to a filesystem via an Ethernet network. This native functionality is the strength of NAS as it provides storage access as a network service. A NAS provides a network filesystem, and does not store data in a host-based, proprietary file system. Data access is governed by the storage controller, and does not require management by a cluster filesystem or host access mechanisms.

The storage object presented by a NAS is the **network file system**, although most Windows administrators may be more familiar with the term **share** or **file share**. We will not be using the latter term in this book as it may confuse the concept of user file sharing with the concept of providing access to hypervisor hosts.

Cloud architects are likely most familiar with the **NFS NAS protocol**; however **SMB (formerly known as CIFS)** is being introduced with the release of **Hyper-v 3.** As of June 2012, most hypervisors support **NFS version 3 (NVSv3)**. While more robust versions of NFS exist, they are yet to be included by the hypervisor vendors. Below is a list of the current NAS protocols supported by major hypervisor platforms.

Below is an image of a shared pool of NAS storage being presented to a cluster of hypervisors.

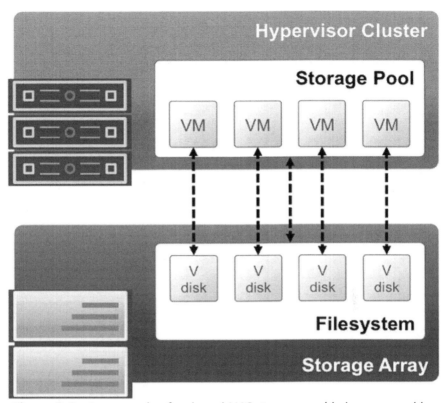

Figure 3-2: *An example of a shared NAS storage pool being accessed by a hypervisor cluster.*

	NFSv3	pNFS	SMB 3.0
VMware vSphere	Yes	No	No
Citrix XenServer	Yes	No	No
Microsoft Hyper-V	No	No	(see below)
Red Hat RHEV	Yes	No	No
Linux KVM	Yes	No	No

Table 3-1: *Hypervisor platforms and supported protocols*

Note: As of June 2012, Microsoft had publicly stated that NAS access via SMB 3.0 will be included with the release of Hyper-v 3 in Windows Server 2012.

Storage Network Fabrics

Hypervisors and shared storage platforms require a storage network in order to communicate and to enable many of their advanced capabilities. Today, the most common storage network fabrics support either **Fibre Channel** or **Ethernet** storage protocols. While other fabric types exist and can be used with many virtualization platforms, like infiniband, we will focus on the most widely deployed forms of storage fabric.

Whether deploying SAN or NAS, the type of existing storage network fabric will limit or expand the storage protocol options available to deploy. Historically speaking, whether comprised of Fibre Channel or Ethernet, it has been the norm for storage networks to be deployed as a separate, second fabric that functioned independently from the core Ethernet networks that supported server and user access. This separation made sense when Fibre Channel and Ethernet could not exist on the same fabric, but this segregation has been unnecessary for some time.

With the advent of **Fibre Channel over Ethernet (FCoE)** and **Datacenter Ethernet (DCE)** this limitation has been removed. While many architects or administrators may profess a preference for separate storage and communication networks, this model is truly limiting. Separate networks result in isolated network resources that cannot be utilized in order to support the requirements of one another.

The deployment of either a Fibre Channel or an Ethernet storage fabric tends to be the crux of the SAN / NAS debate. If an architect deploys a Fibre Channel network, he or she is not just selecting the storage protocol, but deploying separate networking resources. Separate network fabrics result in an increase of network ports, host adapters for connectivity, and a restriction in storage protocol choices.

In short, delaying the convergence of networking fabrics will only increase the networking costs associated with supporting a cloud infrastructure. Separate networks should be converged whenever possible. The table below demonstrates the storage capabilities with each type of network fabric.

	Fibre Channel	**Ethernet**
Shared LUNs	Yes	Yes
LUNs Mapped to VMs	Yes	Yes
Shared NAS	No	Yes
Guest Connected	Yes	Yes

Table 3-2: *Comparing Storage Protocols with Fibre Channel & Ethernet*

The flexibility of Ethernet-based storage protocols significantly outweighs the only option available with a Fibre Channel fabric. Ethernet provides for converged fabrics and a wide range of storage protocols that can provide the most efficient infrastructure, providing the flexibility to deploy a connectivity protocol that best meets the needs of an application or workflow.

Optimizing Fabrics

From a networking perspective, SAN fabrics, whether built on Fibre Channel or Ethernet, are relatively simple to deploy. This statement is not meant to be dismissive of the underlying technologies required to provide high availability, scalability, and security with a SAN. Configuration options such as zoning, LUN masking, VSANs, and ISL trunking are important design considerations that impact storage, but these topics are better addressed as the specific need arises by proprietary networking experts from vendors like Cisco and Brocade.

By contrast, Ethernet NAS fabrics require additional configuration options, and thus are relatively more complex to deploy when compared to a Fibre Channel SAN fabric. While configuration options such as VLANs, port trunking, routing, and flow control are important design considerations that impact storage, they are topics that are best addressed in content published by networking vendors like Cisco, Juniper, and Riverbed.

For the purposes of this chapter, we will focus on basic network topology and multipathing constructs, including physical network links and ports providing connectivity between the hosts in a hypervisor cluster and the storage array

With SAN, an architect should understand that the network fabric provides access, but does not provide path failover, link aggregation, path management, or any other such functionality. These functions are provided by the multipathing solutions available natively within the hypervisor, or with third-party agents from vendors like EMC or Symantec.

With NAS, the fabric provides connectivity, and when using protocols like NFSv3, the storage array and networking devices must provide additional functionality such as path failover, link aggregation, and path management. With Microsoft's introduction of SMB 3.0, some of the requirements of the network to aggregate links and provide failover are significantly reduced.

Storage Performance

Both SAN and NAS based shared storage pools are capable of providing high I/O performance to a VM and to any application it hosts. It is important to consider the impact of the shared infrastructure when running a large volume of VMs and/or performance sensitive datasets within the shared storage pools.

Performance Capabilities

SAN protocols are well understood. As such, they instill confidence in those who select these technologies as they are mature and carry a reputation as being ideal for enterprise-class applications. Historically SANs could be made to provide greater performance than NAS; however when operating as a shared storage pool, the I/O performance of a SAN is regulated by the capabilities of a cluster filesystem.

Beneficially, NAS protocols scale I/O when being accessed by multiple hosts. NAS connectivity is a file-based form of storage access, which means it is free of a number of SCSI-related constructs inherent in a SAN. These SAN constructs require additional technologies like clustered filesystems and multipathing clients to address shared storage. While some architects might question the performance capabilities of NAS, often citing **TCP/IP overhead**, any performance loss due to TCP/IP overhead is equally matched by overhead introduced by the I/O control mechanisms inherent in clustered filesystems.

All SAN and NAS protocols encapsulate the SCSI commands being executed by the VMs running on the hypervisor. Performance is tied to how fluidly the I/O travels through the storage stack. Ultimately, both SAN & NAS protocols operate rather differently, but can provide nearly identical levels of performance.

Note: For further information comparing performance capabilities in a virtual infrastructure refer to the following technical report from VMware & NetApp: TR-3916 Storage Performance: Measuring FCoE, FC, iSCSI, and NFS Protocols (Jafri & Lemmons, 2011).

Ensuring Optimal SAN Performance

It is important to ensure that the storage network has the necessary bandwidth capacity to transmit the required volume of I/O requests. There are a number of factors that can impact I/O performance; however, with modern storage network speeds of ranging from 8Gb to 10Gb, a lack of bandwidth is rarely an issue. There are a number of sophisticated factors that are more often the cause of a bottleneck.

Scaling a Clustered File System

An experienced storage and cloud architect understands the relationship between the number of operations a clustered file system must execute and the number of hosts in the cluster. Often, storage challenges ensue as hypervisor clusters increase in size. Clustered file systems enable the hosts in a cluster to operate in a coordinated fashion through the use of storage mechanisms such as on-disk locking, file locking, SCSI reservations, and reserved ranges of physical storage. As a cluster grows, these constructs can have a negative impact on the overall performance capability of the pool.

Common ways to avoid overwhelming a cluster file system include:

Reducing the operations of the clustered file system by enabling storage hardware offloads such as those available in the **vStorage APIs for Array Integration (VAAI)** from VMware (covered in Chapter 9: Storage Integrations).

Mapping physical storage resources directly to virtual machines, eliminating the need for a clustered file system.

LUN Queues and Path Management

Beyond bandwidth and cluster file system mechanisms, an architect must consider the impact of I/O path management – an often misunderstood topic owing to the dramatic simplification delivered by the most recent technology generation. Modern hypervisors and storage controllers provide support for **Asymmetric Logical Unit Access (ALUA)**, which is an industry-standard method of identifying and accessing the preferred storage paths between hosts and LUNs. When combined with the robust set of multipathing clients that are included in today's hypervisors and operating systems, ALUA delivers a rather intelligent means of ensuring optimal path selection and path availability with no intervention by the administrator.

It is very rare for a virtualized environment to fully capacitate the bandwidth available from modern storage networks; however, it is relatively easy to overwhelm one of the many I/O queues that exist in the SAN I/O stack. This is where the true power of advanced multipathing clients is required to ensure optimal I/O access.

When deploying a large shared pool of SAN storage, a cloud architect needs to be cognizant of the I/O queues within a SAN storage infrastructure. At a high level, I/O queues relate to the number of simultaneous SCSI commands a host HBA/CNA, array target port, and SAN LUN can accommodate.

Should any of the I/O queues in the I/O path become full, all hosts in a hypervisor cluster will receive notification that the queue is full via a **QFULL flow control command**. HBA & CNA ports are relatively large compared to LUN queues, and as long as the I/O load is distributed across multiple target posts, they are difficult to overrun. By contrast, LUN queues are shallow, and so are relatively easy to overrun. Filling an I/O queue will result in reduced overall I/O performance for hosts and the VMs they support until the queue full condition is resolved.

Queue full conditions are relatively common, and result from storage designs focused on consolidating many VMs to a single shared storage resource. By design, these configurations have many more VMs than LUNs. Thus, LUN I/O queues are always at risk of being overwhelmed by the cumulative I/O that can be generated by the multiple VMs being stored and served on them. As such, this state is typically viewed as the performance ceiling of the LUN.

Common ways to avoid address QFULL conditions include:

Reducing the potential to saturate a LUN's queue by reducing the number of VMs residing on the LUN.

Increasing the queue size of the shared storage pool by comprising the pool of multiple LUNs concatenated by a volume manager to support the clustered file system.

Mapping physical storage resources directly to individual virtual machines.

Deploying caching mechanisms that reduce I/O load received by the array, such as host-side caches.

Deploying caching mechanisms that reduce I/O load to the LUN, such as array-side expansion caches and block-sharing aware caches.

Deploying advanced multipathing software that includes path intelligence that will reroute I/O when a QFULL condition exists.

Deploying a shared storage pool accessed via a NAS protocol which does not have the concept of LUNs or LUN queues.

A number of the architectural changes suggested above have trade-offs that must be considered prior to deployment. Reducing the number of VMs per LUN increases operational overhead in areas such as storage provisioning, replication and backup. Managing LUN queues by deploying multiple LUNs, or by mapping LUNs directly to VMs, increases storage provisioning complexity and operational overhead.

Ensuring Optimal NAS Performance

At present, NFSv3 is the dominant version of NAS connectivity implemented in hypervisors. While NFSv3 is high-performing and efficient, it lacks the advanced native multipathing and link aggregation capabilities found in other NAS protocols like NFSv4.1 with pNFS & SMB 3.0. NFSv3 deployments require configuration within the hypervisor, storage array, and network stack to provide bandwidth aggregation and resiliency.

Common items to address in building a robust Ethernet network for NFSv3 include:

Optimized host configurations:

Configure each NAS export or share to an individual IP address - this allows a shared pool to equate to an IP address in a manner similar to the way a LUN has a WWN or iQN.

Ensure multiple Ethernet ports and kernels are configured for storage access.

Enable static load balancing policies on the hypervisor - this step, combined with the previous, will result in the hypervisor utilizing all the Ethernet links designated for NAS connectivity.

Set NIC failover policies.

Disable flow control on the NIC (if possible).

Optimized switch configurations:

Where possible, only use switches that support multi-switch EtherChannel trunking or virtual port channeling.

Enable 802.1Q VLAN trunking with spanning tree portfast.

Disable flow control on these ports (if possible).

Note: Jumbo frames are not necessary with NAS. The use of Jumbo Frames provides modest gains at the expense of increasing network complexity

On the NAS array:

Enable 802.1Q VLAN trunking - static trunking does not provide an appropriate level of redundancy.

Note: Some storage vendors, like EMC & NetApp provide plug-ins for VMware's vCenter Server that automate the configuration process of NFS connectivity, providing a highly resilient and load balanced configuration – these tools address a number of the steps listed above.

Experienced SAN administrators likely won't be impressed with the lack of multipathing intelligence in NFSv3; however, the I/O issues that challenge SAN administrators, like LUN I/O queues, do not exist with NAS. As long as the storage network links aren't saturated, then there is usually no need for link multipathing.

Note: It is our opinion that there is no need to wait for NFSv4.1 with pNFS or SMB 3.0 to deploy a NAS-based solution.

Storage Management of a Shared Storage Pool

The shared storage pool is an ideal design from an operational perspective as it reduces the overall number of storage tasks for the storage admin, and enables the VI admin to consume storage from the pool in demand.

Yet for all its strengths, this model poses some challenges with SAN shared pools in the areas of storage monitoring and management due to the inability to map I/O from the physical resources, through the pool, and to the virtual disk.

NAS provides functionality on par with that of SAN-based shared pools, with the added ability to map and directly access the files on the array as VMs. This correlation between storage objects (virtual disks and NAS files, and shared pools and NAS volumes) provides a form of infrastructure transparency that simplifies storage monitoring and management beyond that found in a SAN-based pool.

Managing Storage Pool Capacity

SAN-Based shared storage pools can have their capacity increased. The process requires coordinated execution by both storage and virtual infrastructure management teams. This process requires a cloud architect to make considerations prior to the expansion of the pool.

If the storage pool is comprised of an individual LUN, its expansion, and the expansion of the clustered file system, is relatively trivial. Before proceeding down this path, a cloud architect should consider whether an increase in capacity will result in an increase in VMs residing in the pool. Increasing the number of VMs residing on the LUN will likely result in an increase in storage I/O requests that may trigger a LUN I/O queue full condition.

If more VMs are destined for the pool, then adding a second LUN, and increasing the overall I/O queue of the pool, may be more appropriate.

The capacity of a NAS storage pool is quite flexible. Increasing or decreasing the capacity of the pool is simple: once the storage administrator makes a change to the size of a storage pool, the virtual infrastructure will apply the change automatically. Some advanced NAS platforms include mechanisms by which capacity can be increased automatically based on utilization policies.

NAS-based pools tend to be significantly larger in capacity, and host a larger number of VMs, than SAN storage pools. By increasing the number of VMs in each NAS pool, the administrator reduces the operational overhead within the environment by reducing the number of procedures associated with administrative tasks like storage provisioning, monitoring, and replication.

Performance Monitoring

It is relatively easy for a storage administrator to monitor the total I/O of a shared SAN pool that it is comprised of a single LUN. Monitoring the cumulative I/O of a pool comprised of multiple LUNs requires more advanced monitoring tools, which are typically provided by the storage vendor.

Regardless of whether a pool is comprised of a single LUN or multiple LUNs, neither model allows the storage admin to correlate the I/O request of a particular VM or particular LUN.

From a storage administrator's perspective, a NAS-Based shared storage pool is monitored differently than that of a SAN-based shared storage pool. With NAS, storage resource monitoring is measured in terms of utilization at the hardware level, such as network link utilization, file system utilization, etc.

Some NAS-based arrays provide I/O monitoring of files that can be correlated and reported as per VM I/O statistics. These capabilities are found in arrays from Sun Microsystems and Tintri.

A virtual infrastructure administrator can monitor the I/O of a shared storage pool and that of an individual virtual disk. The challenge facing the VI admin is that these monitoring tools lack insight into the physical infrastructure. Hypervisor-based tools lack the ability to measure potential issues in devices like LUNs and HBA I/O queues, or performance gains provided by array and host-based caches.

Note: An example of a challenge facing both storage and VI admins includes VM partition misalignment (which is covered in depth in Chapter 2). Native array and hypervisor monitoring tools can monitor and display the I/O of the virtual disk and shared storage pool, but without the ability to correlate the two data points, they are unable to identify conditions in which the array is servicing a greater I/O load than what is being requested by the VM.

Storage Integration with a Shared Storage Pool

There are a number of array-based storage virtualization and integration capabilities available with the SAN- and NAS-based shared storage pools. What a cloud architect needs to understand is that advanced array-based data management capabilities are almost exclusively based on the storage object being presented to the host. Understanding the level of granularity in the integration can provide significant enhancements in deciding which form of storage connectivity best meets an organization's need for a highly capable storage platform.

This means that when deploying a SAN-based shared storage pool, the storage object is a LUN. Thus the ability to create LUN-based snapshot backups, establishing replication relationships, and clone LUNs is really accomplishing these tasks at the shared pool level. For example, a LUN clone would actually be a datastore clone in a VMware vSphere environment.

By contrast, when deploying a NAS-based shared storage pool, the storage object is both a file and a virtual disk device (like VMDKs and VHDs). Thus, the ability to create file- and volume-based snapshot backups, establish replication relationships, and clone files and volumes allows greater flexibility than with a SAN as it allows for completion of these tasks at the VM and/or shared pool level.

A more comprehensive overview of storage integrations is detailed in Chapter 9: Storage Integrations.

Summary and Recommendations

In terms of a making a recommendation concerning the deployment of SAN or NAS, we would like to begin in an indirect manner by enthusiastically endorsing Datacenter Ethernet. The deployment of DCE as a shared network fabric for use with communications and storage needs results in fewer ports, cables, and adapters, and thus provides significant savings while also resulting in a truly flexible networking fabric.

There is no explicitly right or wrong protocol for use in deploying a storage infrastructure for cloud computing. If working with an existing Fibre Channel infrastructure, then deploying over a SAN is likely to be more cost-effective than building a new Ethernet fabric in order to implement a new NAS. However, if an architect has the ability to deploy a 10GbE network, then he or she would be well served to consider NAS. After the initial network configuration, which is more complex than it would be if SAN were used, NAS provides simplicity and manageability that a SAN-based shared storage pool can't match.

Whether you decide to deploy using SAN or NAS, be sure to consider the following strengths and weaknesses:

Strengths of SAN-Based Shared Storage Pools:

Most mid-to-large sized datacenters have existing Fibre Channel and/or Ethernet-based SAN fabrics.

There are more storage platforms on the market today that provide SAN access than NAS.

SAN has more robust multipathing options compared to older and more prevalent NAS offerings in modern hypervisors.

SAN technologies include support for standard block unmap space savings integrations.

SAN is widely supported with integrations from hypervisor vendors.

Challenges with SAN-Based Shared Storage Pools:

There is no native capability to map storage objects to virtual machines.

Granular monitoring and management of virtual disk files on shared pools is difficult.

Supporting separate Fibre Channel and Ethernet networks is inflexible and cost-prohibitive.

Strengths of NAS-Based Shared Storage Pools:

All datacenters, regardless of size, have existing Ethernet based fabrics.

NAS natively maps files to virtual machines for infrastructure transparency.

NAS is Ethernet-based, and thus cost effective & flexible - it allows the addition of SAN protocols, like iSCSI or FCoE, without additional infrastructure expenditures.

NAS is more flexible to manage capacity, and allows for simpler integration and automation.

NAS natively supports multiple hypervisor platforms.

Granular monitoring of virtual disk files is available with some arrays.

NAS is widely supported with integrations from hypervisor vendors.

Challenges with NAS-Based Shared Storage Pools:

Current NAS implementations lack robust multipathing options, thus more complex networking is required - this should change in the future with the release of advance NAS protocols like SMB 3.0.

There are fewer storage platforms offering NAS today than SAN - in addition, many NAS devices are in the form of gateways, which increase the storage solution's hardware footprint and require backend SAN connectivity.

Chapter 4
Guest-Connected
Storage

Guest-Connected Storage

While virtualization is almost universally applicable in the datacenter, there are a number of advanced application configurations and third party integrations for which accessing a virtual disk residing on a shared storage pool is not feasible. For those situations, it is possible to connect storage objects (whether they are LUNs or filesystems) directly to a VM in a manner very similar to the way in which storage objects are connected to a physical server. The authors of this book refer to the various forms of this type of storage connectivity as **guest-connected storage (GCS),** and it is an ideal means to support applications and configurations that cannot normally access a virtual disk.

The practice of connecting storage directly to VMs has had a number of advocates over the years, including the authors of this book. In 2006, we promoted the GCS model as a means to provide storage integration at a VM granular level, and to ensure the highest levels of storage performance. This was our first VMware related publication, *NetApp Technical Report TR-3482: Network Appliance and VMware ESX Server 2.5.x: Building a Virtual Infrastructure from Server to Storage* (Slisinger, Stewart, 2006). Our position has not changed since the publication of that book – directly connecting storage to VMs is the optimal solution for maximized storage performance.

The goal of this chapter is to improve your understanding of GCS, including the various forms available, and to introduce common use cases associated with each, as well as to foster a deeper understanding concerning the strengths and weaknesses found with this type of storage connectivity.

Chapter Contents

This chapter includes the following sections discussing various forms of Guest- Connected Storage, and a summary of its capabilities and best uses:

Benefits & Considerations
Lists a few items of note to consider before implementing

Connecting VMs to a SAN via the Hypervisor
Provides the options for connecting LUNs through the hypervisor to the VM, including the pass-thru and proxy methods

Connecting VMs to SAN & NAS via GOS Initiators
Reviews the connecting of LUNs by a VM without requiring the storage subsystem of a hypervisor

Connecting Applications Directly to NAS Arrays
Reviews the mounting of NAS file systems by a VM or application without requiring the storage subsystem of a hypervisor

Summary and Recommendations
Summarizes the strengths and challenges of the various forms of guest-connected storage

Benefits and Considerations

At a high level, GCS connects storage objects directly to VMs, thus enabling a number of advanced application configurations and third-party integrations that simply aren't available when accessing a virtual disk file. This model of storage connectivity bypasses the shared storage pool and any associated cluster file systems to provide VMs with a means of data access that is very similar to that of physical servers.

GCS is not limited to the mechanisms that connect SAN LUNs directly to VMs. For our purposes GCS also includes the mapping of NAS file systems directly to **guest operating systems (GOS)** and **applications** running within VMs.

Note: In many regards, GCS is similar to the connection between a LUN and a physical server. Interestingly, NAS-based shared storage pools provide storage object awareness between hypervisors and storage platforms, thus they are quite similar in functionality to this mode of GCS. However, this model stands in contrast to a SAN-based shared storage pool, which provides the hypervisor with the ability to manage virtual disks, while in contrast, the storage array is only aware of the LUN or LUNs comprising the storage pool.

Management Considerations with GCS

Later in this chapter, we will present various forms of GCS along with various use cases in which these forms of connectivity produce greater capabilities than what is available from a shared storage pool. However, despite all of the benefits provided by GCS, it is imperative to understand that GCS suffers significantly in manageability at scale.

The first area impacted is operations. GCS mechanisms suffer from a lack of native automation and integration capabilities. The native tools and vendor-led storage integrations tend to be solely focused on the use of shared storage pools. Deploying GCS often results in a one-to-many VM-to-storage object management paradigm. This is the opposite of the management paradigm of shared storage pools, and can result in a prohibitively large number of storage objects to manage.

Hypervisor cluster scalability can also be impacted. The number of LUNs an individual hypervisor can address is finite – commonly limited to 256. In practical terms, this limitation extends beyond the individual hypervisor host, and is actually a cluster-wide limitation that severely impacts the number of LUNs addressable by the cluster, which results in a VM scalability issue.

For example, if a VM requires 4 LUNs then a hypervisor cluster can only host 64 VMs (4 x 64 = 256). An administrator could compensate by creating numerous small-scale clusters, but this architecture would create its own scalability and manageability challenges, so it's important to understand the impact of this manageability complexity before selecting GCS as the default form of storage connectivity.

Some storage platforms and their management applications will be unable to support a large numbers of LUNs. This results from limits on the supported number of LUNs on a selected platform, and / or limits on storage constructs such as the number of replication, snapshot backup, and deduplication operations. Managing thousands or tens of thousands of LUNs is simply not as simple as managing a large volume of files.

Connecting VMs to a SAN via the Hypervisor

The ability to connect LUNs directly to a VM via the hypervisors' storage subsystem has been a storage connectivity option provided by hypervisor vendors for several years. This format of GCS is widely supported by hypervisor vendors, including VMware, Microsoft, Red Hat, Citrix and Oracle and storage vendors including EMC, HP, NetApp and others.

In the past, some architects and administrators viewed GCS as the means to ensure high storage performance for an individual VM. However, any advantages that may have existed have been eliminated with the advancements in storage protocols, cluster file systems, and new data layout practices that resulted from the increases in the number of supported storage pools (wherein a high performance VM can be contained solely in its own storage pool).

A number of advanced storage capabilities provided by hypervisors may not be supported with the use of GCS. For example, vSphere features including **Storage I/O Control (SIOC)** and **Storage Dynamic Resource Scheduler (SDRS)** are not supported with GCS, or as VMware refers to them, **Raw Device Mappings (RDMs)**.

This model of GCS does not provide the ability to dynamically assign LUNs directly to a VM with the default tools provided by hypervisor vendors. This model requires the LUNs to be pre-provisioned and available prior to provisioning VMs. The LUN must be configured for access by all of the nodes in a cluster. The hypervisor maintains a record of the LUN and the VM it is connected to, and the data is transferred over the hypervisor's storage interfaces.

For those seeking a more automated or on-demand storage provisioning model with GCS, third-party tools and automation applications exist today that provide this function with storage arrays that also support on-demand LUN provisioning.

As of August 2012, VMware offered the most robust form of hypervisor-enabled GCS, as vSphere provides both a pass-through and a proxy/virtualized form of connecting LUNs to a VM. Other hypervisors simply provide pass-through connectivity.

In the next section, we will expand on this form of connectivity, and delve into some of the variations available today.

Pass-Through LUN Connectivity

Almost all of today's hypervisor platforms provide a form of support for "Pass-through" SCSI connectivity for connecting LUNs to VMs. This model seems to be the predominant use of this form of GCS for a few reasons: most importantly, the role of the hypervisor is minimal. It uses minimal SCSI virtualization in order to facilitate the connectivity of storage to VMs. As a result, the VM is presented with a LUN, and not a virtual disk.

This mode of connectivity is referred to universally as **pass-through mode,** which simply means the SCSI commands of the guest are passed through the hypervisor and on to the array. In this mode, a VM has the ability to execute array-based capabilities such as application-integrated snapshot-based backup and restore programs, and pointer-based LUN cloning capabilities. Pass-through LUNs often support storage capacities significantly greater than what is possible with virtual disk files.

Below is a list of popular hypervisor platforms, and how pass-through LUN connectivity is referred to with each.

Platform	Pass-Through LUN Connectivity
VMware vSphere	Physical Mode Raw Device Mapping (RDM)
Microsoft Hyper-V	Pass-Through Disk
Red REHV	Direct LUN
Citrix XenServer	Pass-Through Disk (requires the StorageLink adapter)
Oracle OVM	Pass-Through LUN

Table 4-1: *Hypervisor platforms and pass-through LUN connectivity*

A well-known use case that requires Pass-through LUN connectivity is **Microsoft Clustering Services (MSCS)**. Deploying MSCS with VMs residing on separate hypervisors requires direct access to SCSI block storage devices. Pass-through LUNs address this need.

Note: It is possible to directly map SAN & NAS storage from within the VM via a software-based storage initiator that runs from within the GOS or an application. This form of storage connectivity is covered later in this chapter.

Virtual Mode LUN connectivity

VMware offers an alternative means to connect a LUN directly to a VM in which the hypervisor masks the hardware attributes of the LUN from the VM in order to enable hypervisor-provided data management capabilities, like snapshots. One could think of this form as a proxy-based access method. VMware refers to this type of connectivity as a **Virtual Mode Raw Device Mapping**. A Virtual Mode RDM is presented as a direct-attached SCSI virtual disk in the same manner as a file-based **Virtual Machine Disks (VMDKs)**.

Connecting VMs to SAN & NAS via GOS Initiators

An alternative method of connecting storage directly to a VM is to bypass the hypervisor and use the storage initiators and protocols native to the GOS to connect LUNs and file systems directly. The storage connectivity is via Ethernet, thus the available storage protocols are limited to those that support IP. For SAN access, iSCSI is common with all GOS types, whereas the NAS protocols of SMB (or CIFS) are used with Windows, and NFS is used by VMs running Linux. This type of connectivity utilizes the hypervisor's network resources and bypasses its storage subsystem.

Note: while software-based FCoE drivers are readily available, as of August 2012, the support for use within a VM could not be verified.

When connecting LUNs via GOS-based initiators, an administrative user operating within the GOS of a VM controls the storage provisioning and management process, and these operations occur without the involvement of the virtualization team. The storage traffic is viewed as network traffic by the hypervisor. Most of the software-based initiators and protocols include multipathing components, and operate well under production workloads.

Depending on the array capabilities and tools installed in the GOS, the LUN provisioning model may be dynamic, or it may require LUNs to be pre-provisioned. Once connected to a VM, this form of GCS provides significant storage array-based capabilities to the administrators operating within the VM. Examples of these capabilities include executing application-integrated snapshot backups and restore operations, pointer-based storage cloning, and management features like capacity expansion and reduction.

All forms of GCS that communicate via a storage initiator or protocol running within a VM operate without awareness or understanding of the virtual infrastructure. Cloud and application architects need to consider the impact that the use of such forms of SAN connectivity with VMs may place on workflows and automation processes provided by the virtual infrastructure. Examples of areas to investigate include disaster recovery automation, backup software integration and non-disruptive data migration.

For these types of applications, an architect may need to mount a NAS file system directly to a VM (or more likely, a collection of VMs). The use of NAS GCS is typically observed with applications that execute parallel processing operations from many VMs. This is the virtual equivalent of traditional computational grid architecture.

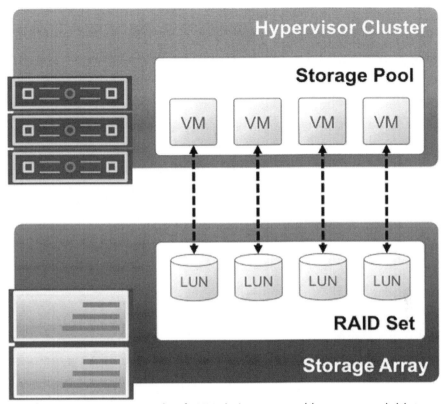

Figure 4-1: *An example of LUNs being mapped by a storage initiator residing within a VM*

Note: As with Pass-through LUNs, Microsoft Clustering Services (MSCS) provides a well-known example of GCS LUNs connected by clients within a VM.

Connecting Applications Directly to NAS Arrays

Recently, some applications have begun to integrate an optimized storage I/O stack. These applications often implement advanced forms of NAS that are tuned specifically to deliver the highest levels of performance, which is often difficult or unachievable by other means. Oracle is the most recognized vendor to embark on this path, with the inclusion of **Direct NFS (dNFS)** in **Oracle Database 11g**.

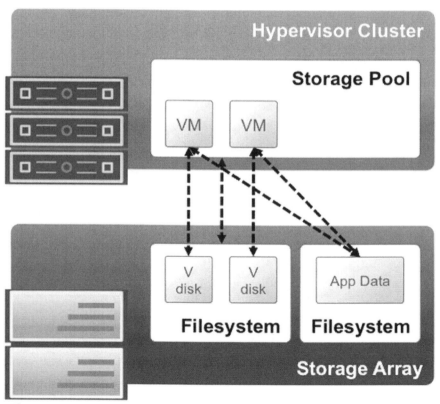

Figure 4-2: *An example of a NAS file system being mapped directly by a VM*

Application-based storage clients bypass both the hypervisor's storage subsystem and also the GOS kernel-level NAS client in the VM. The use of dNFS with virtual instances of Oracle produces extremely high levels of I/O. There are numerous case studies available online for those seeking additional information around this form of GCS.

Note: for some recommended reading on this topic, try "New DNFS Performance Results" by the Oracle Storage Guy at http://oraclestorageguy.typepad.com, the white paper "Oracle Database 11g – Direct NFS Client" by William Hodak and Kevin Closson, found at Oracle.com, or the article "Direct NFS" on the Orafaq.com wiki.

All forms of GCS that communicate via a NAS-enabled application running within a VM operate without awareness or understanding of the virtual infrastructure. Cloud and application architects need to consider the impact that the use of NAS file systems by VMs may place on workflows and automation processes provided by the virtual infrastructure. Examples of such areas to investigate when connecting NAS file systems to VMs include disaster recovery automation, application-specific backup solutions and non-disruptive data migration.

Summary and Recommendations

Guest Connected Storage is a relatively simple way to enhance the storage capabilities of a virtual infrastructure so that it can support additional requirements and applications. The SAN options for GCS include access by the hypervisor and via storage initiators residing within a VM. The SAN forms of GCS provide advanced storage functionality on a VM-granular basis that is otherwise unavailable with virtual disks stored on SAN-based shared storage pools.

GCS also includes support for connecting NAS file systems to VMs and also directly to applications. Together, the use cases for SAN and NAS connectivity provide support for GOS-enabled clustering, grid computing, advanced application capabilities, and integration with functions provided by storage arrays. These are just a few of the strengths associated with the use of GCS.

Even with the limits associated with the shared storage pool model, it is much better suited than other models to provide simple, and easily scalable, storage management solutions for VMs. Today's hypervisor management applications and storage vendor plug-ins lack the policy-driven storage management frameworks to allow for easy scaling with GCS.

There may be a time when hypervisor and storage vendors will improve the ability to better manage scalability issues within the hypervisor, array, and management interfaces that support connecting array-based storage objects directly to VMs. With all of the benefits and advanced capabilities they provide, their use would arguably improve SAN functionality within a virtual infrastructure so that it is closer to the capabilities that exist today with NAS. Until that time comes, it is our recommendation that all forms of GCS connectivity should be used only as required to provide application- or workflow-specific benefits, or to meet infrastructure and performance requirements.

Chapter 5
Storage Saving Technologies

Storage Saving Technologies

The simple premise of "doing more, with less" can be applied to virtual infrastructures and cloud computing: make CPU and memory a shared pool, and over-subscribe physical resources, and you eliminate inefficiencies and overhead; convert manual processes into automated workflows, and the cloud frees operational resources to invest their time in advancing business objectives. Maximized efficiency is the ideological core of cloud computing.

However, this idea is not generally seeing real-life application in regards to storage in virtual infrastructures and cloud computing. While technological advancements have led to massive increases in the capacity requirements of production workloads, the majority of the storage industry is focused on selling the speeds and feeds of "bigger and faster" solutions at the expense of customers' budgets and cloud computing objectives.

A hard reality of datacenter storage is the inevitable discrepancy between advertised physical storage capacity and actual *usable* capacity. The latter is impacted by the overhead requirements of ensuring data accuracy and availability. Compound these necessary inefficiencies with added layers of storage capacity, data that exists after deletion, and other such overhead, and a customer quickly learns that the capacity he or she has purchased is inadequate, despite their pre-overhead estimates indicating the contrary. Storage saving technologies can mitigate this by allowing a customer to store more data on the same physical storage, overcoming some of the inherent inefficiencies of storage solutions. In time, storage saving technologies will become the norm by which data is served within the datacenter. With the advent of "Big Data" they are likely to be one of the defining characteristics of tomorrow's market leaders.

This chapter will focus on reducing storage costs by increasing storage utilization. We will introduce the challenges limiting the efficiency of storage saving technologies, including delving into a number of dependencies and nuances in this area. Once established, we will progress to the assessment of a number of storage saving technologies available within hypervisors and storage array platforms. These reviews include the use of the technologies individually and in combination.

Chapter Sections

This chapter includes the following sections describing multiple storage saving technologies, and how they behave in a cloud environment:

Storage Utilization – the Actual Cost of Storage
Introduces the challenges of obtaining a high rate of storage utilization

Thin Provisioning
An introduction to this technology and its lesser-known caveats

Data Compression & Deduplication
A technical introduction and comparison of these two technologies

Logical Storage Clones
Technical introduction and review

Summary and Recommendations
Summarizes the strengths and challenges of these forms of technologies

Storage Utilization – The Actual Cost of Storage

Traditionally, provisioning storage has required the pre-allocation of physical storage capacity to a host. The provisioned storage capacity is the actual "cost" of storage for that application or data set, regardless of how much or how little data has actually been stored. Achieving higher storage utilization is a means by which an architect can reduce the cost of datacenter operations, but this process is not without its complications.

Storage utilization is often viewed from the perspective of what is being consumed when compared to what has been provisioned. What is missing from this model is the overhead required to protect data from physical errors such as RAID and data consistency checksums. In addition, cloud computing requires that data be stored in a different format, and that format in turn has introduced a new set of challenges around obtaining efficient storage utilization.

As we covered in great depth in previous chapters, the virtual infrastructure uses shared pools of storage to support the actual storing of data in virtual disk files. The result of this architectural model is the introduction of an additional layer in the storage stack, which negatively impacts storage utilization. This layered use of storage produces what we will call the "layered effect on storage utilization."

Understanding this "layered effect" means understanding that measuring storage utilization is complicated, and requires data to be provided from multiple sources.

Consider the view from a storage administrator's perspective: Storage arrays commonly provide data on the consumption of physical storage resources. This basic information is often not enough to justify the need to acquire additional storage capacity. This is not the fault of the storage vendors: the encapsulation of data and use of shared storage pools have broken the mapping of datasets to applications, thus breaking the ability of array-based tools to understand storage consumption, utilization, etc.

Storage teams need help to decipher a report of storage consumption that is based on the amount of storage provisioned. Such reports measure the impact of storage saving technologies like thin provisioning, data deduplication, and compression; however, the data they contain is skewed by items including storage objects that may be provisioned and yet remain empty, or objects containing data which has been deleted.

In addition, storage consumption is reported to an application owner. These individuals reply on tools that reside and run within the guest operating system of a virtual machine, and which provide information about data consumption that often excludes the storage capacity required for storing of data that has been deleted. This contrast in data provided by the reporting tools at the array and application layer can produce challenges in determining true consumption, and thus becomes a challenge for those who measure storage consumption as part of a chargeback model.

Simply put, an architect must understand true storage utilization before he or she can successfully deploy and manage savings technologies and produce meaningful data concerning storage consumption in a cloud architecture.

A simple and universal means to begin to understand true storage utilization is to perform a basic calculation that considers the layered effect of shared storage pools and virtual disks. Many organizations, upon performing this calculation and learning their true storage utilization, will immediately investigate adopting storage saving technologies.

Calculating True Storage Utilization

What follows is an example of the layered effect in a hypothetical, optimal infrastructure. This infrastructure achieves an average storage utilization rate of 70% in all of its virtual disks and across all of its shared storage pools. 70% is an acceptable utilization number, but in a layered environment 70% doesn't *actually* equate to 70%.

By multiplying 70% utilization at one level with 70% utilization at another an administrator discovers a mere 49% storage utilization: hardly optimal. Furthermore, recall that this number is based on usable storage, which is absent of such overhead as RAID protection, data checksums, etc.

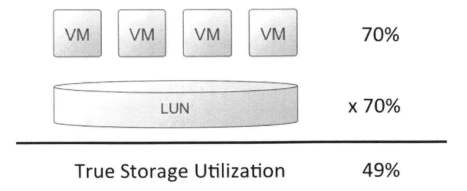

Figure 5-1: *The true storage utilization rate with a shared storage pool*

Historically speaking, storage capacity has almost always been highly underutilized.

There are numerous data points that exist from vendors and analysts that attempt to estimate the actual rate of storage utilization. Useful reports found on websites like informationweek, itworld, and computerworld by authors such as George Crump, Dan Blacharski, and Lucas Mearian (respectively) are readily available, and illustrate the issue clearly. These reports have historically focused on physical server deployments, and do not account for the layered effect. Nonetheless, they will suit our needs for measuring average utilization. When viewed at a macro level, such reports have historically provided data stating that physical servers utilizing DAS and SAN platforms offer average storage utilization levels in the range of 30-45%.

Note: In our previous section, "Calculating True Storage Utilization," our equation was based on average utilization rates of 70% within both the virtual disk files and the shared storage pools. From our experience, most environments are challenged to reach these levels, and operate at rates closer to 60% in the pool and 40% within the virtual disk. These environments operate closer to 24% utilization, which is before any other form of storage overhead.

Traditionally, datacenters have been challenged to maximize their storage investments. How can datacenter architects leverage cloud computing to increase storage savings?

Thin Provisioning

Thin provisioning eliminates the concept of fully pre-provisioning storage objects, and reduces the significant storage overhead associated with traditional (or as we now refer to it, thick) provisioning, instead replacing it with a consume-on-demand storage model. This technology eliminates the provisioned-but-unused "white space" in storage objects, enabling physically shared storage pools to be oversubscribed (or overallocated) in order to increase the actual storage utilization rate, thereby reducing storage costs.

Like thick provisioning, thin provisioning presents a SAN LUN, NAS volume, or virtual disk with a fixed storage capacity. From the perspective of the attached host, there is no difference between a thick or thin provisioned storage object.

Thin provisioning techniques can also be deployed in combination. An administrator can deploy thin virtual disks for his or her virtual servers in thin SAN shared storage pools. This design results in a significant reduction in storage overhead, and allows more data to be stored without having to purchase additional storage capacity.

Limitations of Thin Provisioning

At first glance, this thinly provisioned storage model appears to be very attractive as it eliminates the need to purchase storage in advance of actually storing data; however, there are number of considerations an administrator or architect needs to understand before implementing this technology.

Misconceptions Concerning Data Deletion

The process of deleting data from a file system does not actually result in the data being deleted from the disk. This is not a well-known concept. The process of deleting data results in logical objects being removed from file system tables, but not in the removal of the binary data residing in the file system.

There are benefits to this design, such as the ability to leverage tools that "undelete" data. It is common for modern file systems to implement some form of writing intelligence to avoid overwriting recently deleted data. Each vendor implements this technology in slightly different ways: some use fixed block ranges for each set of data, others only overwrite blocks after all other empty blocks have been written to.

As a result, thin provisioned LUNs and virtual disk files will almost always be larger in size than the amount of data that is currently being presented in the active file system.

As a file system ages, it will eventually reach the state in which every block within that file system has been written to. A traditional storage array cannot tell the difference between a block of active data and a block of deleted data. As such, it only takes time and normal I/O activity to grow a thin provisioned storage object to its maximum capacity.

Some storage arrays and file systems have a process for dealing with this condition (see "space reclamation," below).

IT Operations that Delete Data
There are number of common datacenter operations that delete data as a part of their normal functions. One example is the movement of data, which is actually the combination of copying data and then deleting it from its original location. An example of a data move operation includes migrating virtual disks from one shared storage pool to another, such as occurs within VMware's Storage vMotion. As a result, the thin provisioned shared storage pool will logically increase in available capacity, but will not reduce the amount of storage being consumed on the storage array.

A second example, which usually occurs more frequently than Storage vMotion, is the use of disk defragmentation utilities inside of virtual machines. These utilities attempt to optimize the layout of binary data in the guest's file system. This process can result in a significant percentage of data being moved from its original location to an optimized location. As a result, a thinly provisioned storage object will increase in size.

Storage Utilization Reporting

Data is being continually deleted in a number of fashions when using modern operating systems and file systems. It is very difficult for a storage administrator to explain to a system administrator not only why a storage array is consuming more data than what the system administrator is being informed of by his local file system tools, but also that the discrepancy is comprised of data the system administrator had previously deleted.

The issue of deleted data residing in file systems has led some in the storage industry to label thin provisioning as a "bait and switch" feature, typically delivering exceptional results when first deployed, and then gradually degrading to almost no benefit.

While the "bait and switch" label is not quite fair, it is accurate to say that any environment that uses thin provisioning will have to engage in at least some amount of ongoing maintenance and administration in order to guarantee persistent capacity savings.

Space Reclamation

Space reclamation is the ability to remove data that has been deleted, but which is still stored in the file system of a guest or shared storage pool. Space reclamation allows for thin provisioning technologies to deliver significant storage savings throughout the lifespan of an application, virtual machine, shared storage pool, or storage array.

This capability comes in three forms today; manual processes, storage industry standards, and proprietary storage vendor enablement.

Manual Space Reclamation

Cloud administrators have created a number of rather resourceful means to remove deleted data from within guest file systems. One of the more prominent methods is to use Microsoft's SDelete utility to zero out the deleted blocks in an NTFS file system. Once this process is completed, it can be followed by a Storage VMotion of the virtual disk to another datastore.

The result will be the recovery of storage capacity that was consumed by deleted data within the virtual disk, though this process does not address the data deleted within the shared storage pool. The data that comprised the "bloated" version of the virtual disk will remain after the storage migration is executed. In addition, this process generates a significant amount of storage I/O in order to complete both the zeroing process and the data migration.

Storage Industry Standards

The **International Committee for Information Technology Standards (INCITS)** has established the T10 standard, which provides the ability to unmap blocks on a SCSI block device when blocks are marked as "free" or "deleted" in a file system. The T10 standard applies to SCSI devices specifically, and so its implementation is not applicable to NAS deployments.

By combining the manual space reclamation process along with the storage industry standard T10 for block unmap, it is technically possible to have a method which ensures that thinly provisioned virtual disks and thinly provisioned SAN shared storage pools will only contain live data, and will be free of deleted data.

Note: VMware vSphere supports the ability to unmap deleted blocks from VMFS-formatted datastores as a part of VAAI integration. It does not return blocks from data deleted within the filesystems of VMs.

Proprietary Storage Vendor Enablement

In seeking to improve space reclamation capabilities beyond the manual process required for reclamation inside of a guest file system and beyond the T10 scope of SCSI block devices, some storage vendors are developing their own proprietary technologies.

These efforts are commonly seen in the form of a unified function in which data deleted in the file system of a virtual machine is unmapped on a NAS storage device. There are some significant benefits to this solution: for one, a single process can be executed on a NAS shared storage pool that communicates with the virtual machine guests to identify and reclaim storage, both within the guest and on the storage array. Additionally, this solution is free of the I/O overhead associated with the manual space reclamation process.

Note: NetApp supports the ability to unmap deleted blocks from within NTFS-formatted VMDKs as a part of VSC plug-in for VMware vCenter. This feature is only supported with VMs running on NFS datastores.

Data Compression and Deduplication

Data compression and deduplication are two technologies that reduce the amount of capacity required to store data. Both function well with thin provisioning, and in some use cases also work rather well together. Understanding how each technology works will help a cloud architect implement the appropriate technology for a specific data set or environment.

Data Deduplication

Virtual infrastructures inherently have a high level of data redundancy or commonality. This is the result of consolidating a high volume of virtual machines into a shared storage platform. Simply speaking, Every VM has an OS, and so multiple VMs mean multiple OS deployments, and thus: redundancy. Every OS includes further redundancy provided by the operating system itself. Examples include DLL caches and DLL proliferation with applications installed on more than one VM. Even when the VMs or files like DLLs aren't identical, they often carry a significant amount of redundancy.

Data deduplication is a storage controller capability that reclaims storage by eliminating blocks of redundant binary data that commonly exist on shared storage arrays. Deduplication is designed to increase storage utilization by allowing a given storage medium (disk, array, etc.) to store an amount of logical data greater than its normal physical capacity.

Data deduplication provides storage savings when a dataset shares common data between two stored objects (like those exemplified below). The deduplication process identifies data redundancy in multiple copies, re-points these copies to a single version on-disk, and then reclaims space by deleting the redundant on-disk data. This process results in a reduction in consumed storage capacity without modifying the logical data which constitutes the storage object.

There are many types of datasets which commonly contain redundant data:

Home directories and department shares

Operating system and application binaries within VMs

Email, messaging, and collaboration platforms

Similarly, there are many different, specific implementations of data deduplication technology, including:

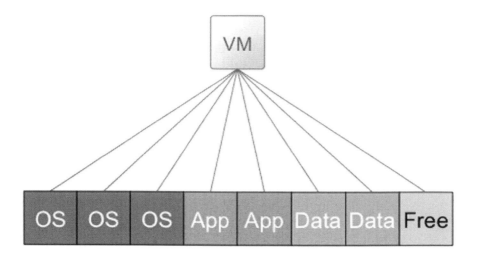

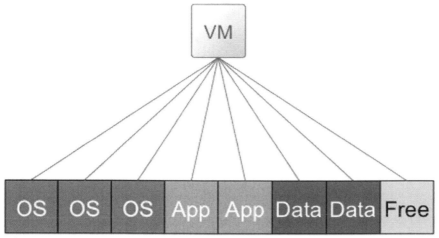

Figure 5-2: *An example of the storage requirements for 2 VMs on an array*

File-Level Deduplication

File-level data deduplication can provide storage savings with unstructured datasets in which a file may be stored multiple times by a user or a group of users. The storage system can identify instances in which multiple versions of the same file exist on disk, and can remove redundant copies while maintaining the ability for users to access the file from the original storage location. File-level data duplication is only available within NAS datasets. Common examples of these types of datasets are user home directories and department or group shares.

Block-Level Deduplication

Block-level data deduplication can provide significantly greater storage savings than file-level data deduplication as block-level deduplication has the ability to remove the redundant blocks that comprise both identical files (just like file-level deduplication) and the redundant portions of non-identical files. Block-level data deduplication supports both SAN and NAS datasets. Common examples of these types of datasets include user home directories, department shares, virtual machines, e-mail and collaboration applications, and backup/archive datasets.

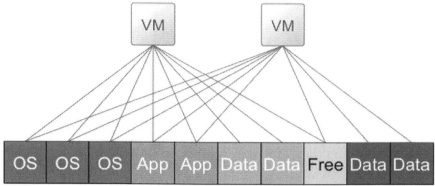

Figure 5-3: *An example of the storage requirements for 2 VMs with block-level deduplicaiton*

Data Compression

Like data deduplication, data compression provides a method for a storage array to reduce the physical storage capacity required to store a given amount of data. Data compression provides storage savings by applying mathematical compression algorithms to the data, resulting in a version of the data that consumes less storage space, but with no change in the data's logical content.

Data compression provides storage savings on data sets that do not have block- or file-level redundancy. Data compression is a viable option in the absence of block-level data deduplication, and is a requirement for many data sets. It should be noted that data compression is the only means to reduce the storage consumption of encrypted datasets and virtual disks.

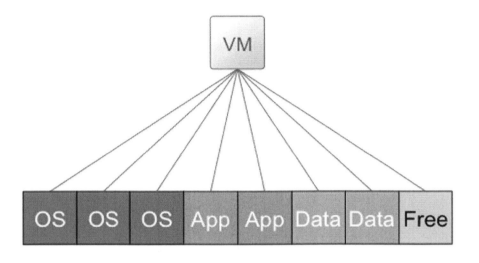

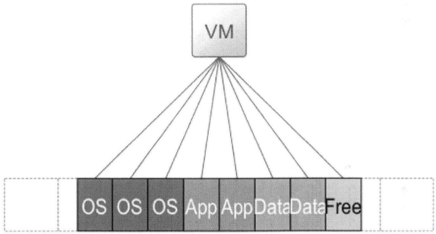

Figure 5-3: *An example of the storage savings resulting from data compression*

There are many different specific implementations of data compression technology, including:

File-level compression
Data compression can provide storage savings when applied to an individual file; however, while this level of granularity appears to provide flexibility, it also requires significant operational overhead, and its use should be discouraged in favor of LUN or volume-level compression.

LUN and File System Compression
LUN- and file-system-level data compression can provide storage savings on large collections of files. One important advantage of this type of compression technology is in the area of management. A storage administrator can simply identify which pools of storage have data compression enabled, and can publish that attribute as part of his or her storage service catalog, or identify these pools manually by using a simple naming convention or other simple management concept.

Use with Production and Backup Datasets
Data compression and deduplication are commonly found on storage arrays specifically designed to store backup or secondary datasets. There is significant value in deduplicating this dataset as there is a high level of redundancy within the dataset itself, as well as redundancy in the multiple copies or versions that are typically maintained online to provide a backup history or archive.

Less commonly, but with increasing frequency, data compression and deduplication are enabled with production workloads. As of August 2012, only a handful of storage vendors provide this type of capability, and the offerings were often limited to a select type of use. Below is a list of well-known implementations of these technologies from a number of storage vendors.

Company	Feature (NAS)	Feature (SAN)
EMC	File-level data deduplication	File and LUN-level deduplication
NetApp	Block level data deduplication, volume and LUN-level compression	Block level data deduplication, volume and LUN-level compression
Nimble Storage		LUN-level compression
Sun Microsystems	Block-level data deduplication	

Table 7-1: *Storage vendors and provided data deduplication and compression technologies*

Enabling data compression and deduplication consumes additional CPU resources, and may impact performance should a system become CPU-bound. Both data compression and deduplication require CPU cycles to store the data in a dense format. Additionally, data compression requires the CPU to uncompress the data at the time of access.

Furthermore, both of these technologies increase the amount of data stored on a disk drive. As a result, the capacity-to-performance ratio increases, resulting in potential performance issues. Both of these technologies should be implemented with caution if the storage array to be used does not provide some form of advanced caching mechanism to compensate for the decrease in performance density.

The value of enabling data compression and deduplication on a production dataset is significant, as the storage savings can have a pervasive effect that results in a decreased storage requirement throughout a datacenter. When production storage requirements have been reduced, there is a correlated reduction in off-site storage requirements for backup, disaster recovery, and distributed high-availability.

Logical Storage Clones

Logical storage cloning is a technology available from both storage array vendors and hypervisor vendors, and is used to provision multiple unique copies of a given storage object (such as a LUN, volume, virtual disk, or file) by allowing each copy to be made off of a source object without the need to completely duplicate the source.

Pointer-Based Array Clones

Some storage vendors have a method for provisioning zero-cost clones of a number of storage objects ranging from entire volumes to individual LUNs and files. This cloning capability can be leveraged in conjunction with a hypervisor for some solutions, and is sometimes integrated directly into the hypervisor itself. A major advantage of hardware-based cloning is that the uniqueness of the clones is maintained within the storage controller, and the storage object clones can be permanently provisioned.

LUN and Volume Clones

When deploying storage in a dense virtual infrastructure, the ability to provide zero-cost LUN and volume clones can aid in reducing both deployment times and required storage capacity. As most cloud deployments use LUNs and volumes as shared storage pools, the ability to clone these objects works particularly well when the solution requires duplication of a large number of virtual machines.

File-Level Clones

File-level cloning provides an obvious benefit to a virtual infrastructure as it replaces cloning of a virtual machine by copying its dataset with a nearly instantaneous and zero-cost hardware clone. Hardware-based file clones provide a storage construct that is very similar to, and in some instances identical to, running block-level data deduplication against a shared storage pool.

The benefit of hardware-enabled file-level clones is that the storage savings and immediate deployment times can be made available for all applications and datasets, including production virtual servers, virtual desktops, and lab test and development.

VMware-Linked Clones

VMware offers logical storage cloning in the form of a software-based linked clone technology. This technology is available in a number of VMware solutions including VMware View, Lab Manager, and vCloud Director.

VMware's technology allows a single virtual machine or template to be used as the base or master image from which multiple clones can be created. As each clone is provisioned, a separate file is created which will log SCSI-level changes that are unique to that clone's virtual disk. As this file is a SCSI change log and not a SCSI-based disk device, this technology is intended to be used for virtual machines that have a temporary or finite lifespan.

Summary and Recommendations

Discrepancies between advertised physical storage capacity and actual usable storage capacity are inevitable. The usable storage capacity provided by a storage platform, whether made up of locally attached disks or a shared storage array, is always going to be less than the raw physical capacity of the devices that comprise the storage system.

In this chapter we discussed a number of reasons for the loss of usable capacity; this includes the various RAID types, disk drive checksums, file system overhead, etc. Despite the virtualization vendors' focus on increased utilization and efficiencies, the gains made in the compute and network layers have yet to reach the storage industry as a whole. In fact, some of the advancements to enable operational savings have resulted in decreased storage utilization (see storage utilization in VMs & clustered file systems as an example).

While storage vendors offer a wide set of storage saving technologies, the results are a mixed bag plagued by inconsistent capabilities and implementations. The well-informed cloud architect can reduce storage costs by achieving higher rates of storage utilization, returning costs savings to their budget, and thus advancing their cloud computing initiatives.

The successful deployment of storage saving technologies is the key. Decreasing storage capacity requirements often results in increased utilization of other resources, like array CPU or disk I/O. Storage savings solution are not a common capability equally available from all solutions in today's market. Architects and administrators should cultivate an awareness of these limitations, similar to the awareness that must be put into practice with the selection of a RAID data protection technology.

Below are some of our recommendations for storage saving technologies that work well within cloud computing environments and virtual infrastructures. These are feature sets which an architect should seek in his or her storage solutions as they provide significant savings, and deliver the performance required for production workloads. We have ranked them in order of priority.

Block-level Data Deduplication & Block-level Data Compression
These types of storage saving technologies, when used with large shared pools of storage, work well in reducing the inherent redundancy found within a virtual infrastructure while providing adequate means to address changes in workload demand. Knowing whether or not these technologies support SAN, NAS or both, and if they can or cannot be used in conjunction within those environments, is essential.

Note: file-level deduplication will not deliver measurable storage savings in structured datasets and virtual machines. It should be avoided in any serious consideration of storage saving technologies for virtual infrastructure.

Solid-state caching

Array caching mechanisms are commonly available in SSD- and DRAM-based cache technologies, and help to provide the performance required for serving production workloads. This technology, while not a storage saving technology itself, is required to compensate for the performance impact of compression and data deduplication. For more information on this technology see the storage tiering section of chapter 6, Storage Performance.

Hardware-Accelerated Virtual Machine & Storage Cloning

Pointer-based virtual machine cloning can provision VMs that are truly block–unique, and which provide immediate, near-zero-storage-consuming VMs. These types of technologies from vendors like EMC & NetApp often have operational boundaries that need to be considered on a use-case by use-case basis.

Thin Provisioning with Space Reclamation

While thin provisioning with space reclamation can result in significant savings, its implementation must be fully understood before it can return maximum value. Thin provisioning allows for storage savings that are often quickly dissipated unless a method to reclaim capacity from deleted data exists. Understanding where and how storage savings are returned is vital.

An ideal solution would incorporate all of these features, but as of August 2012, there are simply too many proprietary and technological hurdles to overcome. A storage architect must make the best decision for his or her organization while acknowledging that such a decision will always be an intelligent compromise. The next chapter will describe the performance of today's storage devices, and should help storage architects and administrators to make the best and most informed choice when choosing storage saving technologies that will complement their chosen storage solutions.

Chapter 6
Storage
Performance

Storage Performance

When evaluating storage array platforms and technologies, many of us are guilty of focusing on published performance results while seeming to forget all about observable real-world performance. The speeds and feeds of an array platform mesmerize us, yet the maximum obtainable performance numbers touted in marketing claims are often difficult, if not downright impossible, to achieve when the technology is deployed in a configuration designed to service a production workload.

The challenges around providing storage services in a cloud infrastructure are compounded when the architect understands that the storage administrator may not have any idea of the workload that will be run inside of the next VM provisioned. Will it be randomly accessed structured data, or sequentially accessed unstructured data? What is the block size? Is the workload throughput or IOPs driven?

So what is possible? How is better performance achieved? Is it simply the result of faster CPUs, solid state disks, and massive volumes of cache? It could be, however, most clouds have financial responsibilities to adhere to, and such a configuration would prove to be monetarily reckless.

This chapter will focus solely on the key components most likely to advance, or limit, an architect's ability to deliver a cost-effective, high performance, and highly integrated storage platform. In doing so, we will cover types of storage media, RAID, caching and tiering.

Chapter Sections

This chapter will discuss the performance characteristics of the components that compromise an I/O stack in the following sections:

Performance Characteristics of Storage Media
Review the performance capabilities of storage media served in a shared configuration

The Performance Impact of RAID
Surveys RAID technologies with a focus on performance

Storage Tiering Concepts
Review storage tiering and caching mechanisms

Summary and Recommendations
The authors' suggestions on improving storage performance

Performance Characteristics of Storage Media

At a fundamental level, a disk drive transfers data from a magnetic medium to the storage I/O bus of an array or computer. A **hard disk drive (HDD)** consists of five key components that enable it to perform its function, namely: *a platter, a spindle, a read/write head, an actuator arm assembly,* and *a controller.*

A typical HDD consists of one or more flat circular disks called *platters*. User-created data is stored on these platters in **binary code (0s and 1s)**. The platter is a rigid, round disk coated with a magnetic material on both the top and bottom surface. Data can be read from, and written to, both surfaces of the platter. The number of platters and the storage capacity of each platter determine the total capacity of the drive.

All the platters are connected to a *spindle*, which in turn is connected to a *motor*, which rotates at a constant speed. Modern disk drives have spindle speeds of 7,200 rpm, 10,000 rpm, and 15,000 rpm (revolutions per minute). These rotational speeds have a correlation with the number of **I/O operations per second (IOPs)** each drive type can deliver. The faster the drive rotates, the less time is required to execute an I/O operation, which results in a greater number of IOPs.

In addition to HDDs, computers use **Solid State Drives (SSDs)**, a form of data storage that uses solid-state memory, commonly in the form of **NAND**, instead of spinning platters. SSDs do not contain moving parts, and thus have lower access and latency times, which in turn result in greater performance capabilities per drive. For all of their capability, SSDs are still relatively new, and have a significant price premium. In addition, they typically support a limited number of writes over the life of the device.

Data Transfer I/O Queues

Requests for data, in the form of **read and write operations**, are transformed to **SCSI commands**. These SCSI commands are exchanged from the vSCSI layer in a virtual machine, to the hypervisor's I/O kernel, then the hypervisor's initiator (HBA, CNA, iSCSI initiator), which has a total queue from which queues for each connected LUN can draw. Once out of the hypervisor, additional queues (or buffers) exist in the fabric switches, and at the array, where the target ports have a shared queue much like the HBA on the host. For some arrays, the LUN will have a queue.

A queue defines the number of simultaneous I/O requests that can be addressed by a device in the I/O path. By queuing or buffering I/O requests, overall storage performance can be increased. However, managing I/O queues can become somewhat tricky with a shared infrastructure. Should an initiator (or more likely, a set of initiators) from a hypervisor cluster send a large volume of I/O requests that overrun any downstream queue, the host will receive a "busy" or "queue full" message that will result in aborted I/O requests and a reduction the storage performance at the application layer.

Below is a list of the I/O queues in the virtualization storage stack:

Queue	Description
vSCSI queues	Queues which are internal to the guest OS – VMs with large I/O requirements should be configured with multiple vSCSI adapters
The hypervisor storage subsystem I/O stack	Introduces an adaptive queue depth algorithm that adjusts the LUN queue depth which in turn adjusts the LUN queue depth based on "busy" or "queue full" messages received by the array (LUN or target port)
Host HBA/CNA or initiator queues*	Include a device-wide queue from which a queue for each connected LUN will be provisioned – most initiators are configured with a per LUN default queue value of 32 and a maximum of 255
Networking Switches	Include queues or buffers - commonly very large and nowhere near as common a concern as compared to host and array based queues
Storage Arrays	Target ports (physical HBAs, CNAs, or software based FCoE or iSCSI ports) which provide a shared port-wide queue - commonly have a queue depth ranging between 1600 and 2048 – does not apply to NFS storage traffic
Storage Arrays (2)	May include I/O queues on a per-LUN basis – usually established based on the number of drives comprising the LUN - may apply to NFS storage traffic where SAN LUNs are provisioned to a NAS gateway
Disk Drive	Queue implemented in controller logic commonly in the form of either **Tagged Command Queuing (TCQ)** or **Native Command Queuing (NCQ).**

Table 8-1: *Queue types and descriptions*

While we may have the storage technology available to obtain the required number of storage IOPs to meet any unexpected spike in demand, it may not always possible due to the number of I/O queues in the I/O path.

The downside to running multiple VMs on shared pools of storage is running into the inherent limits of SCSI constructs such as LUN queues.

In the event that either a LUN or a target port return with a QFULL condition, all I/O from all hosts and VMs stored on the LUN or accessed via the target port will be negatively impacted.

As advances in scaling allow us to deploy larger clusters comprised of a greater number of hypervisors, and store a greater number of VMs per shared storage pool, the likelihood of incurring a queue full condition will increase.

The Performance Impact of RAID

While RAID is covered in greater depth in Chapter 10, RAID Data Protection, we want to remind the reader that RAID technologies have various performance characteristics which are defined by the number of drives in a RAID set, and the number of CPU cycles and disk write operations required to compute and store the data and its accompanying parity information.

We can't afford to overlook the impact of RAID as it is required for production datasets and the protection of the data within, and yet its inclusion reduces the performance of the storage platform in terms of storage capacity and I/O throughput.

The intersection of multiple RAID and disk drive technologies can make a straightforward consideration of RAID storage characteristics somewhat complicated. Just as there is no one single form of RAID, there is no one single RAID performance specification.

RAID sets can offer tremendous value in terms of data protection by mirroring or striping data across numerous physical devices. However, this savings can be offset by the sometimes tremendous storage overhead they incur: continuous parity writes can create chokepoints for data interoperation, and redundant storage can radically decrease overall storage capacity. Additionally, while RAID sets provide native backup utility by creating redundant stripe or mirror datasets, the increase in read and write operations places a greater strain on physical devices, and will cause them to wear out faster.

Nevertheless, the shortcomings of RAID do not outweigh its benefits, and RAID is the de facto standard in virtual datacenter architecture. For more information on RAID and its implementation, see Chapter 10.

Storage Tiering Concepts

Storage tiering involves moving data from one media type to another in order to optimize storage performance and costs. This capability helps ensure that a data set is residing on the most cost effective storage medium based on the I/O requirements of the data set. Tiering provides a means for the storage platform to dynamically adjust to unexpected changes in workloads, which are usually unknown, and often change over the lifecycle of an application.

Storage tiering is commonly implemented by array vendors, either as a cache or as a means to migrate data between various drive types. The tiering mechanism is commonly implemented at a block level (i.e. 4KB) or chunk level (i.e. 1 GB), and often configured at the LUN (sub-LUN or sub-file) or volume level.

Commonly, storage tiering capabilities include the capability to automatically or manually migrate data sets between various forms of storage media non-disruptively within the storage array. For example: the promotion of a data set with a high level of I/O activity from HDD to SSD. The inverse is also possible: the ability to move a data set with light I/O activity residing on high performance drives to a medium more suitable for the application, like from SAS to SATA drives.

Storage tiering is also implemented as a cache, which provides the ability to increase the performance of a data set not by migrating data, but through the implementation of caching algorithms to load the cache in anticipation of future I/O requests.

The Onrush of Host-Side Caches

One method of managing the increase in I/O requests an array must serve is through the deployment of host-side caching mechanisms. These products are often composed of solid state media (often PCIe based DRAM or SSD) and a software filter driver and management application for configuring access of the cache by the VMs.

Caching is a mechanism that transparently stores data in order to serve future I/O requests faster by serving a copy of the data required from a medium that can meet the I/O request with a faster response time. The ability to provide a faster response time to the application or VM is based on the capabilities of the medium and the **round trip time (RTT)** required to respond to the initiator. These capabilities also require software in the form of filter drivers, which require time to process cache content.

By reducing the volume of requests that access data from disk, the array reduces the overall response time per IOP. The greater the number of requests that can be served from cache, the faster the overall response time will be. The array will consequently be able to scale to higher levels, and applications will be able to provide greater performance.

Summary and Recommendations

Server virtualization has dramatically changed the workload of the storage array from what was common just a few years ago. As such, cloud architects need to be aware of the interrelationship between disk drive formats, RAID types, storage tiering, and various caching mechanisms, and how they come together to either optimize or impede the I/O stack.

By reducing the time required to fulfill some of the I/O requests, storage tiering helps the storage array to complete more I/O operations, and thus helps to reduce the number of outstanding requests in an I/O queue.

It is our recommendation that all storage platforms include some form of tiering capability with a bias towards advanced storage caching and the ability to serve structured and unstructured workloads. The application of host-side caches can have a dramatic impact on the performance of certain workloads, but it is important to properly evaluate the application and dataset in use before implementing them.

Chapter 7
Virtual Storage
Arrays

Virtual Storage Arrays

One of the more exciting innovations in the storage industry is the increasing prevalence of **virtual storage arrays** or **virtual storage appliances (VSAs)** in the mainstream market. A virtual storage array transforms the internal direct attached storage (DAS) of a server into a shared storage platform.

The introduction of VSA technology allows architects to use their existing hardware, yet still gain advanced storage capabilities, and with this versatility comes a plethora of new solution offerings. Separating the capabilities of a storage array from any dedicated physical hardware provides the architect with interesting new options that were previously unavailable.

In this chapter, we will introduce you to this new and exciting technology, and discuss some of its use cases. We will also explore ways in which this technology can be integrated into your current storage architecture.

Chapter Sections

This chapter includes the following sections detailing the use of virtual storage arrays in cloud computing:

Introducing the VSA
Reviews the current VSA offerings and its current technical capabilities

High Availability Architectures
Reviews the common method implemented by VSA vendors in order to achieve HA designs

Storage Features & Management
Reviews offerings and decisions points one needs to tackle before purchasing a VSA

Summary and Recommendations
Reviews the current offerings and provides recommends

Introducing the VSA

The architecture of a VSA is comprised of a virtual machine (VM) running on a hypervisor that is running a storage array operating system as the **guest operating system (GOS)**. With physical storage objects assigned to the VSA, the VSA is able to make its storage capacity available as a shared storage platform upon which other VMs or datasets may be stored.

In so doing, VSAs are able to convert inexpensive direct attached storage (DAS) into a shared storage array, and thus enable features that were previously only available from prohibitively expensive dedicated arrays. The resulting configurations are usually lower in cost, and enable new solutions that were previously impossible due to the aforementioned cost, form-factor limitations, and other such considerations.

High Availability Architectures

It is common for VSAs to be deployed in a highly available configuration comprised of either a two-node or a three-node cluster. These configurations require multiple VSAs, each running on a different physical hypervisor. This HA model creates separate failure domains bound to each hypervisor host.

Since VSAs cannot depend on the local storage of the server to be shared between the virtualization hosts, the high availability functionality typically requires that the VSAs establish synchronous replication relationships between the cluster nodes.

In the event that a VSA host fails, the VSA monitoring application will break the mirror on the surviving VSA, and bring the mirrored copy of the storage online. The resiliency inherent in IP-based storage protocols (a combination of long time-out windows and I/O retry requests) provides ample time for the surviving node to assume the IP address of the failed VSA and then send a gratuitous ARP request to redirect traffic to its vNIC.

Two-node clusters will often have a tiebreaker virtual app monitoring both VSAs to ensure avoidance of a split-brain condition in the event of communication loss between the two nodes. The tiebreaker capability is typically inherent in three-node VSA clusters.

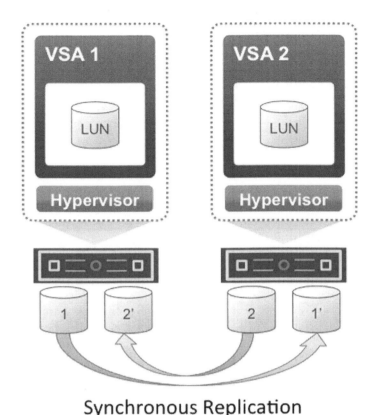

Synchronous Replication

Figure 7-1: *An example of a common VSA HA architecture*

Storage Requirements for HA Designs

HA VSA designs require data to be replicated, or mirrored, between each host. This mechanism addresses the challenges of sharing non-sharable direct attached storage at the expense of storage capacity. This model significantly reduces usable capacity, by 50% with a two-node cluster, and 67% with a three-node cluster.

After accounting for the overhead of the required RAID controller, which could range from 12.5% for a large RAID 5 dataset to 50% for RAID 10, the usable storage capacity of a VSA could range from 43.75% on the high-side to 33.5% in the worst case scenario.

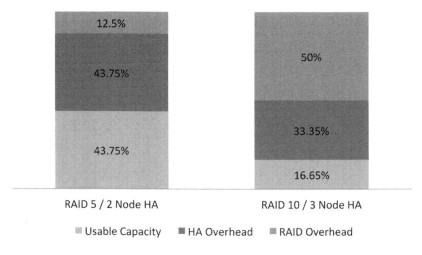

Figure 7-2: *Storage overhead in VSA configurations*

This loss of storage capacity is significant, and results in a substantial increase in overhead to the storage being provided by a VSA platform. In order to preserve the low-cost of a VSA solution, it is imperative that these platforms provide storage savings technologies like data deduplication and compression. Thin provisioning alone is not enough to reverse the capacity lost to the RAID subsystem and the replication required for HA.

Storage Features & Management

VSAs introduce an interesting decision point into architectural designs. When deciding to deploy a VSA, a cloud architect must resolve the manner in which the VSA will interoperate within the infrastructure. Will it interoperate with other storage arrays? Will the storage admin or VI admin team manage it?

Below are just a few thoughts to consider before selecting a VSA:

Storage Protocols & Workloads

VSAs provide shared storage access via software-based IP storage protocols including iSCSI, NFS and SMB. Most of these platforms support a single storage protocol.

A number of vendors offer Virtual Storage Arrays for production workloads including:

Vendor	Virtual Storage Array Product	Protocols
HP	Lefthand Virtual SAN Appliance	iSCSI
NetApp	Data Ontap Edge	iSCSI, NFS, SMB
StorMagic	SvSAN	iSCSI
VMware	vSphere Storage Appliance	NFS

Table 7-1: *Virtual storage array vendors, products, and supported protocols*

Supported Infrastructure

In terms of the systems they support, some VSAs are homogeneous and others are heterogeneous. For example, the VMware vSphere Storage Appliance is only supported in a VMware vSphere environment, whereas VSAs from HP, NetApp and StorMagic support both physical and virtual infrastructures.

Storage Replication

Most VSAs provide some form of storage replication, either between other VSAs or between the VSA and a physical array or multiple physical arrays. All VSAs can leverage software-based replication that operates outside of the VSA, such as hypervisor, host, or application-based means.

VSA	Can Replicate To
StorMagic VSA	StorMagic VSAs
VMware VSA	vSphere hosts on any array with vSphere replication
HP VSA	VSAs and hardware-based arrays
NetApp VSAs	VSAs and hardware-based arrays

Table 7-2: VSA replication compatibilities

Storage Management

It is important to understand which IT operations team will manage a VSA prior to implementation. Should the device be managed by a storage team or by the VI team? Ideally storage teams will want to ensure consistency in their management tools and simplicity in their operational practices, whereas a VI team will likely want to own the device as it runs on a server platform. No single approach is correct in all cases. Discretion on the part of the cloud architect is required.

Storage Savings Technologies

In order to provide high availability from storage resources that are not shared between physical devices, all VSAs replicate their data between multiple nodes. The result of this design is a significant reduction in usable storage capacity, or from another point of view, an increase in storage cost.

The ability to reduce storage requirements by leveraging pointer-based VM clones, data deduplication, and compression can generally restore the costs savings expected from the implementation of VSA platforms. Without these capabilities, the purchase of multiple VSAs for a cluster may be no more cost effective than an entry-level array from a traditional storage vendor.

Points of Integration

Current VSA offerings vary greatly in their support for integrated capabilities from hypervisor and storage vendor-provided tools. Understanding where these capabilities start and stop, and how they are used with physical arrays in the datacenter, may help a cloud architect decide which VSA is appropriate for a deployment.

For example, the vStorage API for Array Integration (VAAI) from VMware is not available on all VSAs listed in this chapter. Another integration example includes application-integrated snapshot-based backups from NetApp. Their VSA operates like an FAS device, and includes this capability.

Summary and Recommendations

We are very excited to see the emergence of the VSA market, and the introduction of the "bring your own hardware" era of storage arrays. The architectural flexibility that a virtual storage array provides offers new options to solve a number of business challenges, and will undoubtedly be used in ways unimagined today. Before an architect decides to deploy VSAs and integrate them into his or her cloud strategy, the true costs and capabilities of these platforms must be understood.

The storage capacity lost to the HA configuration has a significant impact on the total cost of the solution. We recommend that anyone seriously considering deploying a VSA must use a VSA which includes storage saving technologies. Furthermore, a VSA should be able to interoperate with other devices in the infrastructure. Having a greater level of interoperability, and supporting existing datacenter operational models such as storage management interfaces and standardized replication methods, seem to be critical capabilities to successful adoption over the long term.

Chapter 8
Array Virtualization
&
Virtual Storage
Profiles

Array Virtualization & Virtual Storage Profiles

Hypervisors and the virtual machines they host are the means to separate servers and their applications from the constraints of physical devices. This enablement irreversibly changed datacenter operations as it resulted in the ability to dynamically assign hardware resources to a VM over the lifecycle of an application. Virtualized applications received the benefits of infrastructure elasticity, which is essential in operating a cost-effective datacenter.

Virtualizing the hardware access layer of the devices which power the datacenter (above and beyond provisioning VMs) results in a highly dynamic environment that can be adapted to support unexpected changes in workloads and application requirements. Storage array virtualization provides the ability to manage data separate from the restrictions and confines of hardware devices. This technology allows storage administrators to focus on tackling business challenges, as day-to-day storage operations are separated from large-scale, event-driven projects like hardware upgrades and data migrations.

Such capabilities are not the norm with today's physical hardware; however, server, network and storage vendors are certainly heading in that direction. In this chapter, we will introduce you to a number of these technologies within the datacenter, and explore in greater detail how these technologies are realized on storage platforms. We will focus on the strengths of these technologies as they apply to a cloud infrastructure.

Chapter Sections

This chapter includes the following sections, detailing virtual profiles and making recommendations on their implementation:

An Introduction to Virtual Hardware Profile Technologies
A brief overview of virtual profile implementations found in compute and networking platforms

Storage Array Virtualization Technologies
We will discuss the storage capabilities of hardware-based storage virtualization gateways and software-defined virtual storage profiles

Summary and Recommendations
Reviews the current offerings and provides recommends

An Introduction to Virtual Hardware Profile Technologies

With the release of the Unified Computing System (UCS) and Nexus Series Switches, Cisco Systems introduced software-based virtual profile technologies into the server and network markets. These technologies sparked an evolution within these markets as datacenter administrators quickly identified and adopted the value provided by the logical abstraction of a service from a device.

As we will see in this chapter, there are many benefits to be realized from this abstraction. A hypervisor creates a virtualization layer between a server (or VM) and the physical hardware on which it runs. This is advantageous for the administrator, including enabling server portability and allowing the use of disparate hardware. The introduction of virtual profile technology into other layers of the infrastructure stack will give administrators similar flexibility with other datacenter resources. A network administrator will be able to subdivide a physical switch into multiple virtual switches to quickly create new security domains or to defer administration to other groups without purchasing additional physical hardware. A server administrator will be able to rapidly transfer network and Fibre Channel addresses and other configurations between servers when performing swap-outs or hardware upgrades.

Cisco UCS Service Profiles

The Unified Computing System (UCS) introduced the server market to **Service Profiles**, which are a means to encapsulate the identity of a blade server in a virtual profile that can be transferred between physical server devices. These service profiles include elements such as Ethernet and SAN addresses, firmware versions, and boot order. By abstracting the server identity from the hardware layer, service profiles allow hardware changes to occur without impacting other devices or services reliant on communicating with, or monitoring, the server. Examples of such datacenter services include SNMP monitoring, network VLAN assignment and quality-of-service (QoS) policies.

Tasks such as replacing failed hardware or performing hardware upgrades due to asset depreciation or system upgrades are now literally plug-and-play when using service profiles.

Cisco Nexus Virtual Device Context

The **Virtual Device Context (VDC)** provides a form of network hardware virtualization within the Cisco Nexus 7000 switch platform. With VDC, a network administrative team can logically partition the Nexus 7000 into multiple virtual switch devices in order to provide delegated management, fault isolation, service differentiation domains, and adaptive resource management.

The delegated management capabilities of VDCs grant organizations the resources and flexibility to meet their particular and unique business needs while complying with network datacenter policies. Through the use of VDCs, organizations can reduce costs while empowering self-service and management flexibility within their businesses.

Storage Array Virtualization Technologies

Both VDCs and Service Profiles abstract a significant amount of functionality from the hard boundaries of the hardware platform. These technologies enhance the capabilities of an affected hardware platform, making it more dynamic and flexible, or in other words, more in-line with the capabilities of a virtual machine on a hypervisor. Similar capabilities are found in various forms of storage array virtualization technologies.

As of August 2012, there tend to be two predominant types of storage array virtualization: hardware-based storage virtualization gateways, and software-based storage profiles provided natively in storage array platforms. Both of these technologies abstract access to physical storage resources, but accomplish this goal in significantly different ways. There are benefits common to both and values unique to each.

Software-Based Storage Profiles

A software-based storage profile is a native feature to some array controllers, and enables storage virtualization by logically partitioning the attributes normally associated with a physical storage controller. Some storage vendors have referred to their storage profile technologies as a **Global Name Space (GNS)**, which can provide deployment flexibility unavailable when configuring storage resource access to a physical storage array or storage gateway.

A virtual storage profile is flexible, and can be constrained to a single storage controller, or configured to span multiple controllers in a scale-out configuration. Most Storage Profiles / GNS implementations allow the storage administrator team to provide delegated management of the virtual storage profile to a department or organization. This technology is very similar to UCS Service Profiles in that it abstracts the elements of physical storage such as Ethernet and SAN addresses, hostnames, volumes, LUNs, and shares.

By abstracting the identity from the storage hardware layer, storage profiles allow storage objects like shared storage pools or organizational virtual datacenters to remain persistent and unchanged while changes occur at the storage level. This abstraction allows datasets to be tiered not just between disk drive types, but also to be migrated between, or expanded across, multiple storage controllers.

This capability allows the storage administrator to enforce IT data standards around performance and data protection while accelerating the ability of application owners to consume and integrate storage into their service offerings.

The partitioning of a physical array into multiple logical or virtual array profiles is another form of storage virtualization. This partitioning allows the storage controller to provide access to storage resources via software-based storage profiles that are abstracted from physical resources. This model is beneficial because storage services are unbound from the hardware array, and gain flexible attributes similar to those of a VM, a UCS Service Profile, or a Virtual Device Context.

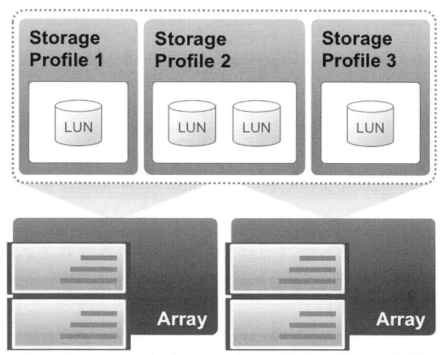

Figure 8-1: *An example of an array cluster with Virtual Storage Profiles*

Virtual storage profiles are available in a number of forms on both array and gateway devices. This includes storage technologies like Global Name Spaces (GNS), and virtual partitioning capabilities in platforms from vendors including HDS and NetApp.

Storage Virtualization Gateways

A Storage Virtualization Gateway is a hardware-based storage controller that provides storage virtualization by acting as a proxy for one or more physical storage controllers. When client or host access has been redirected from physical arrays to the gateway, the dataset being accessed is free to utilize any storage resource that has been assigned to the gateway.

There are a number of benefits to this type of storage virtualization, including the standardization of advanced storage capabilities across a disparate set of storage array platforms. This includes integrations like VAAI, cross-platform replication, and integration into infrastructure orchestration frameworks. Storage gateways can provide new and advanced storage capabilities, such as SAN or NAS services, data deduplication & compression, advanced storage caching and datacenter mobility.

Gateways also provide a means to standardize storage management. The ability to standardize the management tools and operational processes required with a diverse set of storage platforms can be advantageous, particularly in larger environments.

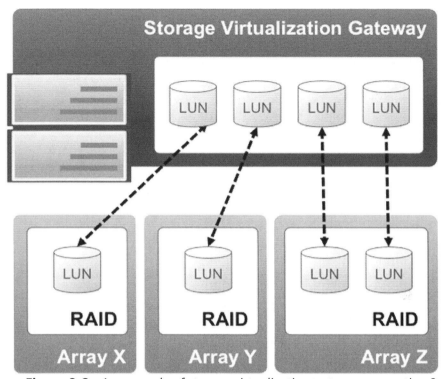

Figure 8-2: *An example of storage virtualization gateway supporting 3 legacy arrays*

Storage virtualization gateways are available from a number of storage vendors, and include platforms such as the SVC by IBM, USP from HDS, the V-Series from NetApp and the VPLEX from EMC.

Note: some gateways offer software-based storage profile functionality.

Drawbacks to the gateway model include the requirement of data migration into the gateway from the source platforms, and the costs associated with purchasing additional hardware in order to provide new enhancements to existing datacenter storage assets.

Summary and Recommendations

Storage array virtualization provides the ability to manage data separate from the restrictions and confines of hardware devices. The means to provide logical access to storage devices simplify day-to-day operations from event driven tasks such as maintenance, hardware refreshes and data migrations.

Whether delivered via a storage gateway device or a software-defined profile, storage virtualization technologies are widely available from almost every mature storage vendor, and are likely on the roadmap for many storage start-ups. There is no debate around the value of this technology; however, one needs to decide between investing in hardware- or software-based solutions.

After reviewing the capabilities of these technologies, it is our recommendation that cloud platforms be served by storage array platforms that natively provide software-based storage profiles. The ability to provide SAN and NAS data access, tenant isolation, delegated management, and the flexibility of software-based configurations without having to purchase a separate hardware platform provides the elasticity, rapid response, agility and costs reductions associated with cloud computing.

Our recommendation is meant to be viewed as a binary decision point that dismisses storage virtualization gateways. These devices provide the significant value to environments that have the burden of technological debt in the form of legacy storage platforms. Gateways can help advance the value in older platforms. If a gateway platform is in your future we recommend you consider those that include software-based storage profiles. This mechanism will allow you to move from gateways to native arrays over the long-term.

Note: This chapter is intended for educational purposes only. It does not imply that all of the vendors mentioned herein offer the same set of capabilities. Please clarify the capabilities of your vendor's storage virtualization gateways, caches, and virtual array partitioning or profile functionality before selecting a technology.

Chapter 9
Storage Integrations

Storage Integrations

Two common benefits associated with private cloud infrastructure are the reduction in the total cost of the infrastructure, and the ability to rapidly meet service requests. In achieving these goals an architect must acknowledge that many of the underlying storage array operations and storage formats are inherently redundant.

When hosts execute a high number of identical commands, or are required to address data beyond the capacity required to complete an operation, the ability of the array, and cloud, to scale and deliver services in an on-demand fashion is reduced.

By integrating a number of data management commands between the hypervisor, guest OS, application, and the storage array, operations complete faster and require fewer infrastructure resources. Both the array and the host scale to greater capacities, and end users receive a more dynamic, on-demand experience.

In this chapter, we will introduce and review a wide range of storage array integrations provided by a number of vendors, spanning hypervisors, applications, and storage. This review will include a generalized overview of these capabilities, and the recommendations at the end of the chapter will attempt to summarize some key points of investigation when deploying these integrations in supporting a cloud infrastructure.

Chapter Sections

In this chapter, we will review a broad set of capabilities enabled via storage integration from hypervisor, storage, and application vendors. These capabilities will be covered in the following sections:

Hypervisor-Enabled Integrations
Explores storage integrations and capabilities provided by hypervisor vendors through standardized sets of APIs

Proprietary Storage Vendor Integrations
An examination of the unique storage vendor-offered platform capabilities that provide enhanced functionality within a virtual infrastructure

Application Vendor Integrations
An examination of the unique application vendor-provided storage integrations and capabilities that provide enhanced scaling and management to the application and administrators

Integrations Benefit Orchestration
Discusses the ways in which hypervisor and storage vendor integrations come together to support automation and orchestration by 3rd party applications

Summary and Recommendations
Reviews storage integrations and offers suggestions for choosing a storage array

Hypervisor-Enabled Integrations

Hypervisor vendors provide a number of advanced storage capabilities designed to optimize the capabilities of storage functions in a virtual infrastructure. These capabilities are provided in two forms: those provided natively by the hypervisor, and those that integrate hypervisor operations for execution by the storage array. These integrations are often provided through a standardized set of APIs or industry standard protocols. When implemented, they provide enhanced storage operations in the support of common datacenter operations.

All hypervisor vendors have a wide and diverse array of storage technology partners, who manufacture a comparably diverse range of storage platforms that support their products. Consequently, the storage integrations the hypervisor vendors develop are often targeted to support a broad range of storage platforms by providing enhancements to common functions, or by addressing widespread challenges found across many or all of those platforms.

To facilitate these integrations, storage vendors receive a standardized set of APIs which they can support by integrating them with their own technologies. However: while the APIs are standardized, the method in which each vendor supports them is truly dependent upon the vendor's proprietary technologies. As such, most of these integrations do not support operations that occur between dissimilar arrays – even those provided by a single vendor.

What follows is a selection of common hypervisor-enabled storage capabilities and integrations, organized by function. These overviews are intended to introduce and explain the indicated capability of each capability or integration: its benefits, its limitations, and its dependencies. Any architect requiring more detailed information on any of the specific technologies discussed should contact his or her hypervisor vendor.

Storage Integrations and Optimizations

The bulk of the integrations provided by hypervisor vendors are targeted at extending the capability of hardware to scale in order to reduce the hardware requirements of a cloud platform. Below is a collection of some of the most prevalent hypervisor integrations. This is not an exhaustive list, nor does it imply that each capability is available from every hypervisor vendor, nor that a capability will be implemented in an identical manner by different storage vendors.

Common Integrations Include:

I/O offload mechanisms
These increase performance by providing a means to offload data copying or modification operations directly to the storage array. These processes are initiated by the hypervisor and executed by the storage array. These capabilities support SAN and NAS arrays.

Enhanced I/O transfers
These enhance storage performance by mapping memory between storage arrays and hypervisors and provide reduced CPU cycles and enhanced I/O transfers. This capability requires RDMA-enabled network adapters in the hypervisor.

Hardware assisted SCSI locking
Advanced atomic locking mechanisms implemented by storage arrays enhance the scaling capabilities of clustered file systems by reducing the number of locks and containing locking to a range of blocks rather than an entire LUN.

Thin provisioned virtual disks
All hypervisors provide this format of virtual disks as a means to reduce the storage required when a VM is deployed.

Thin provisioning space reclamation
The T10 SCSI UNMAP standard allows for the release of data that has been deleted to be returned to the storage subsystem. This capability can operate on clustered file systems and VMs residing on SCSI-based storage, such as SAN arrays.

Assuring storage performance
Dynamic load balancing-mechanisms designed to ensure optimal storage performance for VMs and QOS mechanisms, and to ensure storage performance for VMs in the event of resource contention through storage prioritization policies.

Storage path optimization
Features like asymmetric logical unit access (ALUA) and multipathing policies provide bandwidth aggregation, path resiliency and path optimization for optimized SAN storage connectivity. SMB 3.0 and pNFS provide bandwidth aggregation, path resiliency, and load balancing for NAS storage connectivity.

Note: as of August 2012, pNFS is not available in any shipping hypervisor

Snapshot backup integration
Snapshot integrations provide file system and application consistency for software- and hardware-accelerated backups of virtual machines and the applications they host. This capability is currently limited to NAS deployments.

Backup offload proxies
These tools enable backup applications to better integrate into shared resources, and provide centralized, proxy-based backups for obtaining higher performing backups.

Proprietary Storage Vendor Integrations

Like hypervisor vendors, several storage vendors provide features that enhance virtual infrastructures, VMs, and applications. These features include both common and unique capabilities available when implementing array features into the infrastructure.

Many of these storage-enabled features are delivered via plug-ins into virtual infrastructure management interfaces such as VMware vCenter Server and Microsoft System Center. The plug-in framework bridges the gap between the separate administrative domains of storage and the virtual or cloud infrastructure. Such applications coordinate the integration of the capabilities of a storage array within an infrastructure, application, or OS. These types of features provide market differentiation and uniqueness for the storage vendor.

Examples of such plug-ins that provide integrated storage capabilities such as storage provisioning, cloning, and backups include:

Plug-in	Supported Hypervisors
Dell Management Plug-In for VMware vCenter	vSphere
EMC Virtual Storage Integrator (VSI)	vSphere & Hyper-V
HP Insight Control for VMware vCenter	vSphere
NetApp Virtual Storage Console (VSC)	vSphere & XenServer
NetApp OnCommand Plug-in for Microsoft (OCPM)	Hyper-V
Nimble Storage vCenter Plug-in	vSphere

Table 9-1: *Storage-Vendor plug-ins and their supported* hypervisors

Beyond plug-ins for management tools, there are many very powerful capabilities available in formats such as oVirt, libvirt and the ever-popular Powershell cmdlets, these tools can be used to create advanced scripting and automation solutions to assist with common administration and provisioning tasks.

Storage Integrations and Optimizations

While it is impossible to list all of the proprietary enablements each storage vendor provides to cloud computing environments, below is a collection of some of the most prevalent. As with the common integrations discussed earlier, this list is by no means exhaustive, and should not be read as implying universal availability, nor consistent implementation, between platforms.

Common Integrations Include:

Storage provisioning automation
Provides end-to-end storage provisioning, and the configuration of hypervisor settings to ensure optimal storage availability and performance. These settings include path selection, prioritization and host-side configuration.

Storage capacity management
Allows for the dynamic resizing of the storage and file systems (with SAN) serving as shared storage pools. Shrinking of a shared pool is only available with NAS connectivity.

Storage monitoring
Provides a wide range of valuable data, ranging from I/O statistics to audits of storage connectivity. Some map storage data with that collected by the hypervisor to provide a holistic view of the virtual infrastructure.

I/O Offload
Allows for the copying, migration, and formatting of storage objects without having to route data through the hypervisor. An example of this feature is VM cloning via NAS protocols, using plug-ins and scripts. In addition, storage vendors may be able to further enhance hypervisor vendor integrations by taking advantage of proprietary capabilities.

Correcting partition misalignment
VMs with misaligned partitions suffer performance penalties and increase the storage I/O load that a storage array must support. Some storage vendors provide a function within their storage arrays to address the partition misalignment within VMs in a non-disruptive manner.

Storage saving technologies
Allows for the reduction of storage consumption by providing the means to enable, manage, and report storage savings technologies like data deduplication and compression for LUNs and file systems.

Array-based VM cloning
Provides storage array-based VM clones for hypervisors and applications that don't support I/O offload technologies. These capabilities result in instantaneous, zero-cost VM clones often used in the provisioning of on-demand VMs and desktops.

Array-based snapshot backups
Provides storage array-based snapshot backups for VMs and shared storage pools. These instantaneous hardware-accelerated backups address challenges associated with backing up data using traditional solutions.

Array-based replication
Provides storage array-based data replication capabilities for architectures with backup-to-disk or disaster recovery solutions. These capabilities are often tied to snapshot backups as an automated means to replicate data on a remote storage array.

Application Vendor Integrations

Application and storage vendors offer a rich set of integrations designed to help address the challenges associated with ensuring that application services are not impacted by data management functions. These vendors have found that by integrating with array capabilities, they are better able to manage the ever-increasing requirements around data performance, capacity and availability.

Below is a collection of some of the most prevalent integrations. As with the lists above, this selection is necessarily truncated, and by no means exhaustive. Your vendor(s) can give you a more complete picture of integration availability.

Common Integrations Include:

Array-based VM cloning
Provides storage array-based VM clones. Applications commonly implement these capabilities in areas like test and development. The application can automate the process and development life cycle of a virtual machine (or group of machines) from provisioning to promotion and deployment to production use.

For multi-tier applications, it is common for the test and development environment to be exponentially larger than production. The ability to create zero-cost storage clones can significantly reduce storage requirements for these environments.

Array-based snapshot backups
Provides storage array-based snapshot backups for VMs and shared storage pools. These instantaneous hardware-accelerated backups address specific challenges associated with backing up large sets of data.

For tier-1 applications that implement their own form of replication, integrating snapshot backups eliminates the need to reseed all data after a failover event. Application-integrated checkpoints allow data resynchronization to be reduced to only the data generated since the last checkpoint or snapshot. This enablement may save days or weeks of data replication, depending on the capacity being addressed.

Integrations Benefit Orchestration

Arguably, what defines an infrastructure as a cloud deployment is the ability of the infrastructure to deliver resources and services on-demand, in an automated fashion. This is where infrastructure orchestration and workflow automation applications bridge the needs of the virtual infrastructure to the consumers of these services. Many well-known virtualization vendors provide such orchestration and automation suites, including VMware and Microsoft. However, there are also a number of cross-platform applications provided by vendors and foundations like Cloupia, Gale Technologies, CA, and OpenStack, to name just a few.

The key to powering such automation resides in the ability of orchestration applications to interoperate with the software and hardware infrastructure components. Taking advantage of these best-of-breed application-specific orchestration solutions provides the best results in terms of service automation and delivery. Unfortunately, a single management framework that can address all of the use-case needs of the datacenter is rare, especially as one seeks automation that is hardware-specific or supports multiple hypervisors.

While it is perfectly reasonable to address the automation of different service areas and applications separately today, architects should plan for a future in which all of these datacenter resources will regularly interact. Integrations such as those covered in this chapter will help to provide process simplification and execution standardization.

By choosing management solutions that are API-controllable, and thus include a wide set of integration capabilities, the datacenter architect will create service offerings that can to fit a wide range of management frameworks, and deliver a truly virtual software-driven datacenter.

Summary and Recommendations

Cloud architects must understand the broad range of technologies and integration capabilities available at all layers of the cloud infrastructure spanning the hypervisor, network, guest OS, application, and storage. Clearly, significant structure and value are delivered to the infrastructure in both standardized and non-standardized models. However, these technologies are not available in all storage arrays, nor are they implemented in the same manner across array vendors and / or multiple platforms from any one individual array vendor.

When choosing a storage array, we recommend you look for these significant feature sets:

First: That the array vendor provides substantial integration with hypervisor APIs. Allowing for storage functions to be a native operation within the hypervisor's workflow simplifies the architect's task of implementing these capabilities. This includes hypervisor APIs like VAAI, and emerging standards like the capabilities in the SMB 3.0 protocol.

Next: That the array vendor provides substantial integration with application APIs. By allowing for storage functions to be a native operation within the application, storage architects can defer application-specific decisions and operations to the administrators of those applications. This simplifies the storage architecture's capacity to scale across an entire organization, and is critical to addressing challenges associated with today's rampant data growth.

Next: That the array vendor provides API functionality in an open and well-adopted format, so that the orchestration and automation of functions beyond hypervisor-enabled capabilities will be possible. In this area, the authors recommend (when appropriate) Powershell Cmdlets as they are broadly supported in hypervisors, network, compute, GOS, applications, and storage platforms.

Finally: That the array vendor provides these integrations in a standardized manner across their product line. Where possible, an array feature should provide the same benefits regardless of platform or protocol. This ability allows a cloud architect to leverage different models of hardware arrays, taking advantage of the different performance and capacity capabilities of the hardware without the worry of reduced functionality.

Some of the capabilities described above can be found in the form of software enablement provided by the hypervisor. These should be considered before committing to a specific architecture. A thoughtful architect will attempt to pair hypervisor solutions with storage arrays so that the features of each will compliment the other, maximizing capabilities and compensating for deficiencies.

Chapter 10
RAID Data
Protection

RAID Data Protection

In designing datacenter architectures, there is one constant that applies to all technologies, platforms, and operations: the inevitability of component failure. However – the market by and large has not applied a critical perspective to data protection technologies and the impact of storage component failure in a shared, virtual cloud architecture.

The virtual infrastructure underlying cloud computing is based on leveraging shared hardware infrastructures which support a significantly greater number of datacenter services than their traditional, physical predecessors. The impact of a storage component failure in a traditional datacenter was in some ways modest: the negative impact to operations was constrained to an individual application or, in the case of a large-scale application like an email server environment, limited to a subset of services or users.

The impact of a failure within a shared, virtual infrastructure can be catastrophic for an organization, business, or service provider, and potentially career ending for the architect who does not design the appropriate level of data protection.

This chapter includes a review of the most common data protection technologies available in the market, which we examine with an emphasis on how well they address the needs of a virtual infrastructure. By the end of this chapter, you should have a solid understanding of these technologies, and how their combined usage provides the foundation for datacenter operations and integration into business continuance plans.

Chapter Sections

This chapter contains the following sections, explaining data storage failures and the use of RAID in minimizing their impact:

How and Why Devices Fail

Explains bit error rates and failure types in a network and on solid state data storage devices

The Likelihood of a Failure

Considers factors by which failure can be considered "likely," and what that means for data architecture

RAID Technologies in-Depth

Compares the availability, performance, and cost of the RAID type spectrum

Calculating the Risk

Explores the determining factors in evaluating risk preparedness

The Impact of a Drive Failure on a Cloud

Explains the real consequences of drive failure in a cloud infrastructure

Summary and Recommendations

The significant key points of this chapter

How and Why Devices Fail

Building a highly available storage platform requires redundancy at the physical infrastructure and data communications layer. The technologies required at both of these levels span the array, storage fabric, and host configurations, and require a number of capabilities including multipathing agents and application redundancies. Before anyone can dive into these high-level means of delivering availability, we need to begin with a basic construct – data protection. The scope of this chapter is limited to a review of the common, currently available RAID technologies.

Every disk drive, regardless of type or manufacturer, is comprised of media imperfections, and will incur failures for a number of reasons, ranging from the operational wear on moving parts to media life cycle limits. There are also less well-known issues such as the **bathtub curve**, a principle which demonstrates that the highest failure rates of a device either occur with drives early in the manufacturing lifecycle, or in operation near the end of the physical device's lifetime.

Bit Error Rates

As disk drive storage capacities have consistently increased, and the deployment of large capacity shared storage pools becomes more common, datasets are increasingly being exposed to a growing number of media imperfections. Together, these factors result in reduced reliability of the storage medium. This correlation is true for both rotational and solid-state disk drives.

The reliability of rotational disk drives is determined by two factors: disk drive type (discussed below) and non-recoverable read errors per bits read. Most refer to the latter as the **bit error rate (BER)**. With a quick glance at the website of any disk drive vendor, it is easy to see that the BER of modern low-capacity, high-performance drives, including SCSI, SAS, and SSD SAS average a BER of 1 in every 10^16 bits.

> *"The observed range of [**Annualized Failure Rates**] (**AFRs**) varies from 1.7%, for drives that were in their first year of operation, to over 8.6%, observed in the 3-year old population" from Google Research:* Failure Trends in a Large Disk Drive Population (Pinheiro, Weber, Barroso, 2008)

By contrast, modern high-capacity, low-performance disk drives such as SATA average a BER of 1 in every 10^15 bits. This is an exponentially higher BER than that of the low capacity, high performance drives. Considering that the high-capacity drives store a great many more bits than the high-performance drives, the error rate is much more significant.

Cell Failure in Solid State Drives

There is a misconception that because Solid State Drives (SSDs) lack moving parts, they are more reliable than rotational disk drives. The reality is that SSDs are significantly more complex than rotational disk drives, and this complexity can lead to device failure.

SSDs are comprised of cells, pages, and blocks (which in turn make up planes and dies, though this is beyond the needs of this example). In simple terms, NAND flash stores data in cells, and in order to enable NAND to be addressed as a disk device, those cells are grouped into pages that act in a manner similar to that of block in a rotating drive.

The NAND media in storage devices like SSDs have a finite number of **program and erase (P/E) cycles**. This limit is due to the degradation of the oxide layer that makes up the physical memory media. The number of P/E cycles can vary based on the type of SSD. The following ranges are commonly agreed upon P/E cycle limits per SSD type:

SSD Type	P/E Cycle Limit
SLC NAND SSDs	commonly average 100,000 P/E cycles
MLC NAND SSDs	commonly average 3,000-5,000 P/E cycles
eMLC NAND SSDs	commonly average 20,000-30,000 P/E cycles

Table 10-1: *P/E cycle limits per SSD type.*

Modern eMLC SSDs typically require 32,768 NAND cells to compose an 8KB page - 8KB pages have recently succeeded the previous common page size of 4KB, which are composed of 16,384 cells. It is possible for the failure of an individual cell to cause the loss of data within an 8KB page. SSD manufacturers and storage array vendors have incorporated a number of technologies and practices, like error correction codes and data checksums, which are designed to reduce the number of P/E cycles, thereby helping to ensure data integrity.

It is common for SSD arrays that implement these wear-leveling technologies to experience mass cell failures as the SSD Drives approach their P/E cycle limit in unison. Since the wear is spread around across multiple cells, all cells approach a critical mass of decay together, rather than small batches of cells failing in sequence throughout the life of the storage device.

Because of their complexity as it pertains to the potential for total page failure, SSD Drives should not be considered as reliable as their high-speed, low-capacity rotating media counterparts with their lower BERs.

The Likelihood of a Failure

Relative to many devices we interact with in our day-to-day lives, the failure and error rates of disk drives are minuscule – practically non-existent. Comparing the number of operations performed by an SSD as compared to the number of operations performed by an automobile can give us some perspective: the SSD will complete billions of P/E cycles over its life span – an automobile is good for a few thousand trips to the grocery store. In the cosmic sense, this math should be reassuring.

However, such comparative math does not reflect the realities of datacenter supply and demand.

Demand consistently outpaces supply – an SSD that can perform billions of P/E cycles will, by the end of its lifetime (the right end of the bathtub curve) be expected to perform tens of billions. Its next-gen replacement will flawlessly execute tens of billions of P/E cycles when deployed, but will be obsolete when replaced, eclipsed by devices that can perform trillions of P/E cycles.

The volume of stored data increases at an astounding rate. Far from satiating organizational needs for data retention, increased storage capacity has only fueled users' appetites for eternal archives of data on-demand. This increasing workload magnifies the infinitesimally small risk of device failure by a catastrophic magnitude: the device that can perform millions of operations can and will fail when called upon to perform billions.

All failure rates are magnified by the sheer volume of data that devices store – we will mathematically explore the likelihood of failure in short order. However: regardless of likelihood, RAID technologies can help to mitigate this risk.

RAID Technologies in-Depth

RAID is an acronym for **Redundant Array of Independent Disks**. RAID provides data protection by producing redundancy in the data set. From this redundancy, data can be reconstructed should the RAID group incur a loss of media. The number of simultaneous losses a RAID type can survive varies based on the form of RAID technology.

Each form of RAID requires differing quantities of storage capacity overhead to provide data protection. This has a direct impact on the total cost of the storage as the capacity used to ensure data protection is unusable. This can be thought of as a data protection tax – a portion of space which cannot be used for storage, but which ensures storage security.

In addition to these storage costs, all RAID technologies implement a unique means to calculate and store data redundantly. As such, it is important to understand when, how, and if additional storage I/O operations occur, and how they impact the I/O process.

There are three fundamental attributes to be considered before deploying RAID. These attributes directly inform any form of RAID's usefulness to a virtual infrastructure. These attributes are:

Availability – the ability to ensure data availability in the face of one or more hardware failures.

Performance – the level of performance available to meet the I/O requirements of the production workload.

Cost – the amount of hardware overhead required to ensure availability.

In an ideal cloud deployment, the RAID technology used would optimize all three attributes. Availability and performance are critical in servicing multiple virtual machines stored on large shared pools of storage, and the ability to do so while remaining cost-effective will be a determining factor in any solution.

There are many types of RAID protection technologies. This section will focus on the most widely deployed. The following sub-section evaluates a number of common RAID technologies, and how well they meet the needs of a virtual infrastructure.

RAID 0

RAID level 0, commonly referred to as **data striping**, involves writing data across all disks in the RAID set, and requires a minimum of two drives to implement. This RAID level is commonly used to provide very high performance volumes for transient data, as this level offers no data protection.

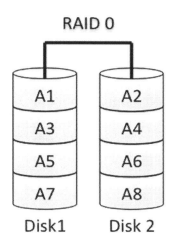

Figure 10-1: *RAID level 0*

Consequently, the use of RAID 0 is not recommended within a virtual infrastructure. Both cloud administrators and hypervisor data management constructs have the ability to move critical workloads on to this unprotected data set. In this scenario, a storage failure would be catastrophic.

RAID 1

RAID level 1 is commonly referred to as **data mirroring,** and is normally implemented with two drives. This level is considered fault tolerant in that if a single drive fails, the surviving drive can continue to service I/O requests as it is an identical copy of the failed one. Mirroring enables the storage system to continue functioning uninterrupted until the failed drive is replaced.

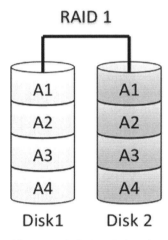

Figure 10-2: *RAID level 1*

RAID 1 has the lowest storage efficiency, or in other words, the highest storage costs, of any form of RAID. For this reason, it is rarely used in cloud deployments. Beyond the cost, this format provides fair performance as both drives service I/O requests without the need to calculate parity. RAID 1 provides data protection in the event of a single drive failure, and no protection in the event of a multiple-drive failure.

Considering the high cost of storage, and the limited level of data protection in the event of multiple disk failures, RAID 1 is not recommended for use within a virtual infrastructure.

RAID 5

RAID level 5 is currently the most commonly deployed form of RAID. RAID 5 became prominent with the advent of open systems like UNIX and Windows, and its use has carried over into virtual infrastructures. This industry-wide popularity is likely the result of the high correlation of virtual infrastructure administrators with backgrounds in open systems administration.

RAID 5 is also known as **block-level striping with distributed parity**. Parity data allows for data from a failed block or drive to be reconstructed in the event of a failure. The reconstruction is done by comparing the data from the surviving drives in the RAID set. The data protection provided by the parity data will reduce the overall storage capacity of the RAID set. Based on common deployment configurations ranging from 4 to 8 drives, the overhead will range from 14 to 33%. A RAID 5 set will survive the failure of a single member of the set, but if a second member of the set should fail during that time, data will be lost. RAID 5 requires a minimum of three drives, and is most commonly deployed in RAID group sizes of 4, 5, and 8 disk drives.

The parity computational process results in data and parity data being written to all of the disk drives in the RAID set. Simply put, RAID 5 doubles the write operations required to store data. The first write stores the data and the second provides the parity data. As a result, the write performance of RAID 5 is considered moderate.

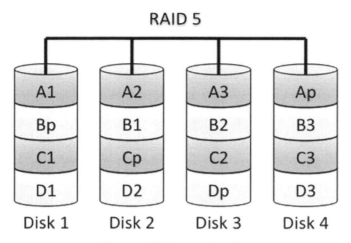

Figure 10-3: *RAID level 5*

RAID 5 gained prominence with the emergence of open systems in the 1990s. It provided adequate data protection at relatively low storage price. On the surface, the low cost of RAID 5 may seem appealing; however, due to the moderate performance capabilities and low level of data protection, we cannot recommend its use within a virtual infrastructure.

RAID 6

RAID level 6 is a superset or an extension of RAID 5. RAID 6 can be described as **block-level striping with double-distributed parity**. RAID 6 uses parity in a method similar to RAID 5, but RAID 6 performs a second parity calculation. This increases the data protection overhead, but significantly increases the reliability of the RAID set, including the ability to survive two simultaneous drive failures – furthermore, the considerable data protection overhead can be offset by using larger RAID group sizes.   By using larger RAID group sizes, RAID 6 can deliver superior data protection than RAID 5, at the same level of data protection overhead. RAID 6 requires a minimum of three drives, and is most commonly deployed in RAID group size of 10, 12, and 16 disk drives.

In the same fashion as its predecessor, the parity computational process of RAID 6 results in data and parity data being written to all of the disk drives in the RAID set. RAID 6 invokes triple write operations in order to store data. The first write stores the actual data, and the second and third writes provide the first and second set of parity data. As a result, the write performance of RAID 6 is considered poor.

RAID 6 provides a superior level of data protection as it provides continued data access in the event of the failure of two drives within the RAID set. By comparison, all previously discussed RAID levels only support the failure of a single drive.

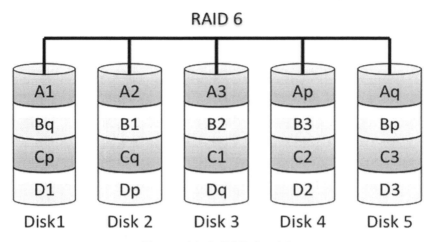

Figure 10-4: *RAID level 6*

RAID 6 provides a low-cost form of data protection that provides high availability and moderate performance (high reads, poor writes). The performance of RAID 6 can be further improved if the storage platform utilizes solid-state media as a write cache, thus compensating for the weakest attribute of this technology. The use of a write-optimized implementation of RAID 6 is recommended with cloud architectures.

RAID 10 and RAID 0+1

RAID level 10 and its close cousin, RAID 0+1, are implemented by layering RAID 1 and RAID 0 in combination. The result of these RAID technologies is high I/O performance, and data resiliency that supports the failure of multiple disk drives.

These two RAID types function in rather similar ways: RAID 10 stripes data (RAID 0) across a number of mirrored RAID 1 sets; by comparison, RAID 0+1 implements a mirrored configuration (RAID 1) of two striped RAID 0 sets. Both approaches require a minimum of four drives.

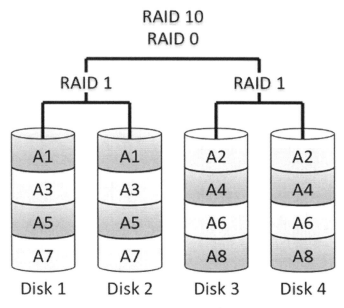

Figure 10-5: *RAID level 10*

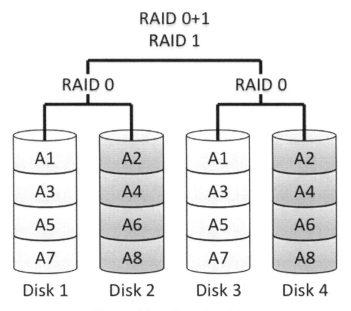

Figure 10-6: *RAID level 0+1*

Both formats offer a high level of performance by combining the speeds of RAID 0 with the resiliency of RAID 1 without requiring the parity calculations associated with the other RAID levels.

As both RAID 10 and RAID 0+1 implement data mirroring, they require 100% storage overhead to provide data protection, which increases storage costs, and makes both forms too expensive for cloud computing infrastructures.

RAID-DP

RAID-DP is considered a form of RAID 6 by SNIA definition and its vendor, NetApp. RAID-DP can be thought of as **block-level striping with centralized double parity**.

RAID-DP is the only proprietary form of RAID we considered for inclusion in this chapter. It is our view that RAID-DP is likely the most widely deployed proprietary form of RAID technology.

Disclaimer: as of August 2012, and as is mentioned in the introduction, both authors are employed by NetApp. The inclusion of RAID-DP is not meant to be a commercial endorsement of this technology, but an invitation for architects to consider the merits of this protocol.

RAID-DP implements parity to provide a storage-efficient means of data protection. RAID-DP requires a minimum of three drives, and is most commonly deployed in RAID group sizes ranging from 14 to 28 drives.

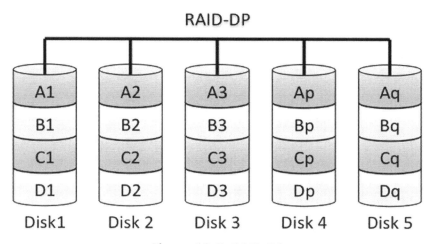

Figure 10-7: *RAID-DP*

Like RAID 6, RAID-DP protects against the simultaneous failure of two drives within a RAID set. However, unlike RAID 6, RAID-DP writes this parity data to disk drives dedicated to storing parity data. As a result, RAID-DP can execute a write operation that delivers data and parity data to a RAID set as a single write operation. Consequently, the write performance of RAID-DP is considered high. It should be noted that all NetApp storage platforms include solid state NVRAM that acts as a write cache. The NVRAM cache acknowledges write-upon-receipt, which is to say it is able to safely commit a write and acknowledge that fact to a host before the data is actually written to disk.

RAID-DP provides a high level of data protection and performance at a very low cost of implementation. Like RAID 6, the use of RAID-DP is recommended with cloud architectures.

Calculating the Risk

It is relatively easy to understand the risks facing a dataset by the application of a simple mathematical equation to the freely available specifications published by disk drive manufacturers. For simplicity's sake, we will demonstrate the risk factor for data loss based on a set of disk drives deployed with a RAID technology that provides data protection in the event of a single drive failure.

The most common form of RAID which provides this level of data protection is RAID 5 – the most widely deployed form of RAID with open system platforms and virtual cloud infrastructures. With any form of RAID, data can be reconstructed from parity data stored on the disks in the RAID groups so long as there is only a single failure. Failure types include SSD cell rot, encountering a bit error, or the loss of the physical drive.

As we have discussed throughout this work, the requirements of the modern cloud infrastructure may demand new capabilities than what has been traditionally expected of some common technologies. Traditional RAID data protection schemes have been used to protect datasets from the failure of individual disk drives. As we will see below, the virtual infrastructure demands that we now address the possibility of multiple drive failures.

Complete simultaneous failures of two physical disk drives within a RAID set are rare. This is a testament to the reliability of disk drives. The larger and more common issue that plagues administrators and architects is an inability to retrieve data from a parity set in a degraded RAID group. Below is a list of common failure scenarios:

While reconstructing a failed block, the recovery process is interrupted by a failed cell or bit error in another block, and is unable to complete.

While recovering from a failed drive, the recovery process encounters a failed cell or bit error on a surviving drive and is unable to complete.

While recovering from a failed drive, another drive fails completely, and the recovery process is unable to complete.

In all of these scenarios, the reconstruction operation fails because the RAID-level cannot support more than a single failure, and data is lost.

To calculate the actual risk of failure for a given physical device, visit the web site of any disk drive vendor, select a disk drive, and note its capacity and BER. Then, apply that drive's configuration to a common RAID configuration, such as a RAID 5 4+1 configuration, which is a common deployment, and which is used in the example below.

For this example, we will deploy five 3TB SATA hard drives protected in a conservative RAID 5 4+1 configuration. For the sake of mathematics, we convert the drive from gigabytes to bits (as BERs are provided by the vendors in bytes).

The formula to calculate the likelihood of encountering two simultaneous media failures is as follows:

Surviving drives	Multiplied by	3TBs capacity each	Multiply to convert	Terabytes to bits	Divide by	BER
4	x	3,000,000,000,000	x	8	÷	10^15
= 9.6% failure rate						

Figure 10-8: *Example likelihood of encountering two simultaneous media failures in four 3TB SATA hard drives*

Based on vendor-provided documentation, a modern 7,200RPM SATA drive, configured in a 4+1 RAID 5 configuration runs a 9.6% chance of losing data during a RAID reconstruction operation.

This same formula works just as well for high-performance SAS drives as it does on 7,200 RPM SATAs. SAS drives are exponentially more resilient, and provide a fraction of the storage capacity, and as such it is common practice for these devices to be configured in a moderately conservative RAID 5 7+1 configuration.

The equation for this configuration is:

Surviving drives	Multiplied by	6GBs capacity each	Multiply to convert	Gigabytes to bits	Divide by	BER
7	x	600,000,000,000	x	8	÷	10^16
= .34% failure rate						

Figure 10-9: *Example likelihood of encountering two simultaneous media failures in seven 600GB high-performance SAS drives*

Evidently, the risk factor decreases significantly. Does this mean SAS drives are acceptable? Maybe. There is a correlating reduction in overall storage capacity and a number of other items that are addressed further along in this chapter.

Considering the number of VMs running on each RAID group, it is helpful to place this data in the context of a virtual infrastructure. For example, the SAS RAID group offers approximately 4TB of usable capacity, and so could host 10, 15, even 20 VMs. The individual architect must determine an acceptable level of data loss based on density: many datacenters strive to achieve 99.999% uptime. To meet this uptime requirement, a solution can only experience 5.26 minutes of downtime per year. Given the very real chance of data loss from just a single drive failure, we can see that many RAID technologies are inadequate to meeting these uptime requirements.

Alternately, the SATA configuration could store a significantly greater number of VMs with its 12 TBs of usable storage, but there is a radically greater chance of data loss.

The Impact of a Drive Failure on a Cloud

Formats like RAID5, RAID6 and RAID-DP implement parity mechanisms to provide space-efficient data redundancy. The downside to parity-based implementations is the impact on the storage controller when a data reconstruction process is invoked.

While statistically speaking it may be highly unlikely to have two disk drives fail simultaneously, a single disk failure is rather likely to incur a media error, or failed block, on another disk drive during the RAID data reconstruction process.

During a RAID reconstruction processes, the I/O load on the surviving drives and the CPU of the array are significantly increased as data is recalculated from the surviving data and parity data, and written to a new drive. During this time, the data protection for the affected RAID group is reduced, and will not return to its normal operational state until the reconstruction operation completes.

Due to the reduced level of data protection during reconstruction, it is imperative that the storage array complete the reconstruction process as quickly as possible. Thus it is fairly common for arrays to be negatively impacted by the significant increase in I/O load during reconstruction. The continuing increase in demand upon storage supply further complicates matters: increasing storage capacity density lengthens the time required to complete RAID reconstruction operations, thus increasing the window of reduced protection and performance.

As if demand were not high enough, unintended data migrations initiated by storage I/O mechanisms like SIOC and Storage DRS in vSphere can increase I/O load during a reconstruction operation. These operations only add to the already increased I/O on an array, resulting in even longer periods of impaired operational state.

It is important to note that rebuild times vary greatly and depend on a number of factors including current production workload, drive type and rotational speed, drive capacity (size) and RAID set size.

Avoiding the Impact of RAID Reconstruction

Most enterprise-class storage arrays include the means to actively track drive errors, and have the ability to proactively identify and remove less than reliable drives based on a set of reliability factors and error count thresholds. This capability results in most drives being proactively failed by the system prior to the drive experiencing a physical failure.

Some storage vendors have expanded upon the monitoring and proactive failing capabilities of such storage arrays, and have provided a means to eliminate the need to execute a RAID reconstruction in all but the most edge-case scenarios. These platforms utilize the aforementioned reliability systems as the means to proactively duplicate the data of the unreliable drive to a spare drive, which upon completion of the copy operation will replace the failed drive.

The process of copying data from one drive to another does increase the overall disk I/O operations on the array, however this increase is significantly less than a reconstruction, and is limited to the unreliable drive and its eventual replacement. This process allows the array to both address a failing drive without reducing data protection, and to avoid the increased I/O and CPU load associated with a RAID reconstruction operation. Consequently, RAID reconstruction avoidance technologies should be a requirement of any storage platform being considered.

Summary and Recommendations

Choosing the right RAID data protection technology is critical to successfully meeting the I/O workload and data protection requirements of a virtual cloud infrastructure.

RAID technologies which provide data protection in the event of a single drive failure simply aren't reliable enough to support the scale of a modern cloud deployment. Equally ill suited are RAID technologies that mirror data, as they are simply too inefficient, and as a result, too expensive, to be realistically considered for implementation.

Raid Type	Usable Capacity	Cost	Data Protection	Speed
RAID 0	100%	Low	NONE	High
RAID 1	50%	High	Medium	Medium-Low
RAID 5	75%	Low-Medium	Medium	Medium
RAID 6	50%	High	High	Medium-Low
RAID 10 & 0+1	50%	High	Medium	High
RAID-DP	87.5%	Low	High	High

Table 10-2: *Appraisal of RAID capabilities in a virtual environment*

It is our recommendation that cloud platforms should only deploy RAID technologies that protect data in the event of simultaneous component failures, and which can do so via space-efficient parity sets. RAID 6 and the proprietary RAID-DP are ideal for dense, highly available, yet cost-effective deployments. Both of these RAID formats require some form of solid state write cache in order to ensure high performance: NetApp implements NVRAM as their write buffer, and most RAID 6 implementations use SSD in a similar fashion. These types of offerings include vendors like EMC, Nimble Storage, and Sun Microsystems.

Chapter 11
Backup and
Disaster Recovery

Backup and Disaster Recovery

Cloud architects are increasingly seeking new ways to enhance and expand the scope of their business continuance capabilities in order to keep up with the growing demands of organizations on their virtual infrastructures. Challenges such as the sheer capacity of data to handle (aka "big data") and shared hardware are driving these architects to seek more agile and flexible approaches to business continuance – approaches that are both simple to manage, and which also introduce greater levels of automation and resilience than were available in the past.

The need to protect data and services within a datacenter is well understood. Through data protection processes such as backup and disaster recovery (DR), organizations are protected from operational loss due to events such as human error or infrastructure failure. The latter can range from hardware failures to natural and manmade disasters.

Simply put, backup and disaster recovery are unfortunately necessary contingencies in modern datacenter operations. The majority of the traditional data protection processes and applications in operation today were designed for use with physical servers. Traditional backup and DR infrastructures are hard-pressed to support cloud computing platforms, failing (by most metrics) to meet an organization's **recovery time objectives (RTO)**.

In this chapter, we will evaluate modern backup and disaster recovery options in terms of how well these technologies work in restoring services in a cloud infrastructure.

Chapter Sections

This chapter examines the challenges of, and unique capabilities provided by, virtual infrastructures in the areas of backup and disaster recovery. This will include a review of backup and disaster recovery technologies and operational processes that are better suited to meet the business continuity goals of a cloud infrastructure:

Restoring Services versus Recovering Data
Introduces the challenges facing backing up virtual infrastructure

Business Continuity Basics
Discusses of the goals of backup and disaster recovery functions – introduces related concepts such as RPO and RTO

Common Backup Mediums
Compares and contrasts the capabilities of tape libraries, virtual tape libraries, and storage array disk

Common Backup Formats
Evaluates some of the strengths and weaknesses of guest-based backups, image-based backups, array-based snapshot backups, and continuous data protection

Data Replication
Surveys the data copy methods between media

Disaster Recovery Automation

An introduction to this technology and its lesser-known caveats

Summary and Recommendations
Bringing backup and disaster recovery together

Restoring Services versus Recovering Data

Datacenter architects and administrators, along with the datacenters they design and operate, are more than distributors and stockers of data: they are also its guardians. Whether by operator error, malfeasance, mechanical failure, or acts of god, data faces a number of threats, and threats to data are threats to the very life and health of any datacenter, and to the organization which it supports.

As dynamic and flexible as a cloud infrastructure is, it presents challenges to the datacenter architect in securing and storing data, and in optimizing uptime in the event of a disaster. The same versatility that allows virtualized environments to share compute and storage resources can result in crippling I/O bottlenecks when an architect attempts to implement traditional backup models in large cloud environments.

Regardless, data protection, and by proxy, data recovery, is at the forefront of the architect's responsibilities; however, recovery is not the goal – the goal is the restoration of the services the data provide. This is a key distinction, one which we will emphasize throughout this chapter. Fortunately, backup technology is advancing at a reasonably comparable pace to virtualization, but now those responsible for backup need to also manage service availability.

Business Continuity Basics

Before we discuss technologies, we need to establish a set of mutually understood objectives with backup and disaster recovery processes. We will do so in lay terms in an attempt to best represent a broad set of technologies.

Recovery Point Objective (RPO)

One of the key measurements of a backup Service Level Agreement (SLA), the **RPO** represents the maximum window of time in which data could be permanently lost. RPOs are calculated by measuring the maximum amount of time between two backup recovery points.

Example:

A 4-hour RPO indicates that the point in time recovered to after a failure could be as great as 4 hours prior to the failure. This would mean that a database could, in the event of a failure, lose as much as 4 hours' worth of transactions.

The RPO requirements for a given dataset will generally have a significant effect on the technology requirements of its data protection solution.

Recovery Time Objective (RTO)

Another key measurement of a backup SLA, the RTO is the maximum amount of time required to restore a data set or application to its normal operational state following a failure. It is common for important applications to have an RTO measured in seconds or minutes. Backup applications are used in coordination with clustering and disk replication capabilities to meet these RTO goals.

Example:

If an application has a 2 hour RTO, this means that it will be expected to take 2 hours or less to recover that application after a failure.

Like the RPO, RTO requirements have a significant impact on the technology requirements of a solution.

Backup

The basic function of backup applications is to produce copies of data sets to be accessed in the event that the original source data is lost or invalidated. Traditionally, tape has been the primary medium used to store backup data sets. Disk-based backup technologies can complement or replace tape-based solutions.

Backup solutions require backup software packages in order to copy data from the production source to the backup media. These applications provide data and application consistency along with operational management frameworks.

Regardless of the components deployed in a backup solution, the following functions must be provided:

The ability to restore a complete copy of the dataset

Store backup data on a physical medium separate from the medium storing production data

Backup data should reside in a separate geographical location than the location of the production data.

Disaster Recovery

Disaster recovery (DR) is a process designed to provide datacenter services in the event that the production infrastructure becomes unavailable. Most DR designs provide minimal service disruption, and require adequate redundant infrastructure to reside in locations geographically separate from the production location. Designing DR plans requires careful considerations of application deployment and availability options, and of the volume of data to replicate or restore, as well as DR validation exercises to ensure that these plans will operate in the event of an issue.

Disaster Avoidance

An important emerging business continuance strategy is **disaster avoidance**. This concept of disaster avoidance involves non-disruptively migrating datacenter services to another datacenter in advance of an expected outage at the production datacenter. Disaster avoidance employs advanced data mobility capabilities, and requires virtual infrastructure, networking, and storage technologies. The storage technologies that support disaster avoidance include stretched clusters and geographically spanned storage caches. These technologies are covered in greater depth in Chapter 12: Datacenter Mobility and Enhanced Availability.

Common Backup Mediums

Disk, tape, or both in tandem are all viable storage media to be deployed in a backup architecture. Each is described below.

Tape Libraries

The tried and true datacenter backup media is magnetic tape. It is used in nearly every datacenter in production today, either directly or indirectly, in the form of traditional, physical, or virtual tape libraries. With high-performing data transfer rates available at a price point that is less expensive than disk drives, the main drawback to the use of tape is that it has a sole utility: offline data storage.

The offline aspect of how tape stores data severely impedes its ability to restore services to an operational state in a timely manner. First, tape offers a copy-based restore process. In the event of a complete VM loss, an administrator must wait for data to be restored in full before services can be restored. This limitation is exacerbated when the restore process is asked to handle large sets of data, such as those found with large applications or a large number of VMs.

Virtualization enables the restoration of services with data that can be immediately accessed, and as such, tape is better suited for long-term archiving than for backup in a virtual infrastructure.

Virtual Tape Libraries

From within a backup application, **Virtual Tape Libraries (VTL)** function no differently than tape-based backups. At a high level, a VTL is a disk array that presents itself as a tape device to a backup media server. The ability of VTLs to non-disruptively join a traditional backup solution has played a tremendous part in the popularity of this technology. To reduce backup and restore times, VTLs store data on disk in sequence, and then provide a means to export backup data to magnetic tape.

From a cloud perspective, VTLs provide significant performance gains in restoring data; however, they face the same single-purpose functionality restrictions found with magnetic tape. The administrator must wait for data to be restored prior to access, regardless of whether the data is stored on disk or tape.

Storage Array Disk

Storing backup data directly on disk is relatively straightforward. Disk arrays tend to provide backup media in two forms; storage array-based snapshot backups, and backup applications writing to disk storage targets.

Array-based snapshot backups are often implemented in the form of reserved disk space residing on the same physical disk and array as the production data set. Thus snapshot reserves provide a short-term repository of recovery points and require the data to be transferred to another form of media, like tape or backup disk targets, for long-term retention.

Disk-based backup targets are often found in the form of storage arrays optimized for storing data in a highly space-efficient manner. They often include the ability to deduplicate and compress data at a block level.

Both storage array disk solutions and snapshots and disk targets support direct access to data in the event of a restore. Thus applications that preserve the format of the VM's virtual disk can provide the ability to serve data directly from these backup storage resources providing a nearly instantaneous restore capability. Once the VM is running, and the services are available to users, the data can be non-disruptively migrated through hypervisor mechanisms like VMware's Storage vMotion.

Common Backup Formats

With the advent of cloud computing, many architects and administrators have sought to optimize their backup solutions through the implementation of new backup processes and technologies. The goal is to find the method which completes the backup process is a timeframe that can be achieved daily, and which provides the proper set of restore capabilities. Beyond these basic goals, architects needs to consider data growth rates, and how the backup process will be able to scale in order to meet future demands.

Below are a few of the most common backup mechanisms. Each offers its own advantages and disadvantages when addressing the challenge of backing up VMs and the data encapsulated in virtual disk files.

Guest-Based Backups

In a virtualized environment, traditional tape backup solutions commonly operate no differently than they do with physical servers. This model is attractive since it results in no change to backup operations as compared to a traditional environment. Administrative processes, backup granularity, and application support are unaware that the data being backed up resides within a VM. It is for this reason alone that guest-based backups remain the most common form of backup solutions deployed with server virtualization.

These backup applications usually require that a backup agent be installed inside of the Guest Operating System (GOS) of the virtual machine (VM). These agents rely on a central backup service to provide them their operational conditions such as backup schedule, backup targets, data to exclude, etc. This method places the responsibility for the backup within the VM itself, resulting in increased CPU, memory, and disk load on the VM, hypervisor, and shared infrastructure.

Guest-based backups usually store their backup data on tape libraries, disk-arrays, or the hybrid **virtual tape libraries (VTL)**. Normally, guest backup applications require data to be copied in whole, as a **full backup**, on a recurring basis. These backup applications introduce scalability challenges, especially with larger deployments, as the volume of data being copied en masse can overwhelm the I/O capabilities of the shared infrastructure.

Note: To put this challenge into perspective, consider that a tape-based backup protecting a single transaction in a SQL database requires the entire database to be copied to tape. Thus an 8KB transaction record could result in hundreds of gigabytes of data being transferred for backup purposes.

Any form of large I/O transfers, such as those resulting from a backup application, runs the risk of overtaxing the storage infrastructure resources, which may unintentionally trigger load-balancing mechanisms provided by the hypervisor or performance mechanisms within a storage array (like storage tiering). This could result in additional I/O load on an already stressed infrastructure, resulting in even larger performance problems and the inability to complete backups in the required timeframe.

Guest-based backups provide file- and VM-level restore capabilities. This form of backup often requires the data to be retrieved from the backup set and restored to disk before it can be accessed should an entire VM or set of VMs need to be restored

Image-Based Backups

As virtual machines are comprised of collections of files, it is possible to complete a backup by simply copying those files. This model is considered an **image backup**. These operations often coordinate the copy activity with an agent installed within the VM, which provides file system, and in some cases application, consistency. Some image-based backup software applications implement storage saving technologies that include the means to reduce the amount of storage consumed with each backup.

The advantage to image-based backups is that resources of the VM will generally not participate in the backup process, thus ensuring minimal, if any, impact on the CPU and memory performance of the VM. Disk performance may be impacted due to the storage mechanisms of the hypervisor. A common culprit includes SCSI-based transaction logs, which provide the mechanism to prevent data writes to the virtual disk while the backup operation is being executed. Advancements have been made in this area to reduce this overhead by using mechanisms like changed block tracking, which reduces the performance impact during backup activities, but may introduce extra storage load during normal times of operation.

Image-level backups store their backup sets on disk. From these disks, the backups may be subsequently copied off to tape for long-term archival purposes. As many of the image-based backup solutions focus solely on storing data on disk, a second backup application that supports tape drives and libraries to handle the archival process is often required.

Image-based backups provide both file- and VM-level restore capabilities. As they are image-based, and preserve the virtual disk format, they often require a proxy mechanism for file restorations. They also provide a significant advantage in the area of VM level restores as the combination of the backup format and the backup medium allows the backup images to be immediately restored without the requirement of copying data. This results in a nearly immediate restoration of services, which can be followed by a non-disruptive data copying process like VMware's Storage vMotion.

Array-Based Snapshot Backups

Array-Based Snapshot Backups offer an advanced form of image-based backup by replacing the software-based data copy and SCSI block tracking mechanisms of the hypervisor with hardware-accelerated pointer-based snapshots within the storage array. This method completes image-based backups through the creation of a local recovery point (snapshot), which is subsequently available to be replicated to another storage array or sent to tape.

The ability to create recovery points that are not dependent on the time required to transfer data to another form of media for completion means that the array-based snapshot backup method provides for RPOs that can't be realized with guest-based or image-based backup solutions. Snapshot backups are stored in an unmodified format on disk (enabling advanced recovery models), and may provide additional uses to support business operations. By combining snapshots with array-based cloning technologies, snapshots can be used as the data repository for test and development, data mining and analytics, and disaster recovery testing.

Array-based snapshot backups provide file- and VM-level restore capabilities. As they are image-based, and preserve the virtual disk format, they often require a proxy mechanism for file restorations. They also provide a significant advantage in the area of VM-level restores as the combination of the backup format and the backup medium allows the backup images to be immediately restored without the requirement of copying data, resulting in a nearly immediate restoration of services. Unlike the software form of image-based backups, snapshots are local to the production disk, and so the restoration of a VM can usually be completed without having to copy data from a secondary set of disks; however, should this copy be required, the restoration from remote disk can be followed by a non-disruptive data copying process like VMware's Storage vMotion.

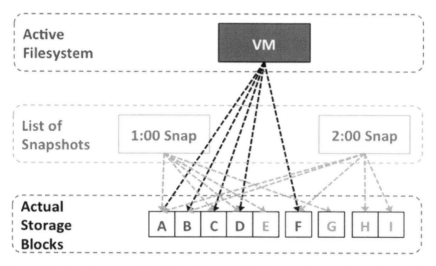

Figure 11-1: *An example of the storage efficiency of array-based snapshot backups*

Note: Array-based snapshots can often be integrated into application-based replication solutions to provide on-disk consistency points. The advantage of this capability is that it eliminates the need to re-baseline an application's data in the event of a failure. Snapshot technology can be used to replicate new data written during the recovery period to the failed node once the node has been returned to service.

Snapshot backups are a function of the storage array, and must be triggered by a backup application that supports them. The capabilities of these applications vary widely, so be sure that you are aware of the capabilities and limitations of your backup software before making a purchasing decision. Backup applications that do not natively support array snapshots can usually be augmented by user-provided scripts. Your storage vendor may already have some of these scripts available.

Continuous Data Protection

Continuous data protection (CDP) is a hybrid form of backup and replication. It implements a data replication mechanism in the storage fabric that tracks changed blocks in a local storage pool or cache from which data replication services are provided. This architecture provides heterogeneous (cross-platform and vendor) array replication.

CDP promises data recovery from any point in time as long as that point in time exists in the local storage pool. Recovery to a specific time is not possible if that recovery point has been flushed from the cache. CDP requires additional datacenter resources to be deployed to support the computational and storage overhead of the CDP servers. These resources are required in every facility that is a part of the CDP solution, and resource requirements may vary based on the amount of data being tracked and transferred.

CDP provides the ability to roll back VMs and the files within them to a previous point in time. The remote replica of the data can also be accessed as a means to restore services should the primary disk array be unavailable. In the event of this condition, CDP replication can be invoked in reverse to resynchronize the data, and then services can be returned to the production site with a simple reboot of the VM.

Data Replication

The ability to replicate data between two or more storage devices is required for the implementation of disaster recovery capabilities, and for architects and administrators wishing to store array-based snapshots on disk arrays for archive purposes. There are a number of data replication options available, ranging from software-based applications to hardware-based solutions found both natively and outside of the capabilities of deployed storage arrays.

Application-Based Replication

Application-based replication is the standard means by which modern tier-1 applications are deployed in highly available, and often geographically dispersed, configurations. A common means of replication is based on transaction logs replicated to one or more servers, which are replayed and applied to the stand-by copies in remote locations. These log-shipping solutions often support more than one replica in a high availability design.

The benefit of application-based replication is the speed at which services are made available when a node is lost. As such, application-based replication solutions have a place in any DR plan, but the overhead associated with these solutions will mean that they are best applied to tier-1 applications. Since non-tier-1 applications and services will usually represent more than 80% of the data in a modern datacenter, another replication solution will have to be selected as well.

Host-Based Replication

Host-based replication is software that runs either on the hypervisor or within the **guest operating system (GOS)** of a VM. These technologies replicate data at a block level between similar hypervisors or operating systems. The benefit of this technology is that it is "hardware-agnostic," and may (depending on vendor and configuration) store and transfer the data in a compressed format. This functionality may be included natively in some hypervisor platforms and operating systems. 3rd party replication applications are also available.

For the flexibility it provides, host-based replication does pose a few challenges. It may place an increased load on the physical resources of the host hypervisor, it may lack support for applications, and it may only support data running on the hypervisor, thus requiring different replication technologies for the rest of the systems in the datacenter. As discussed earlier in this chapter, stressing resources of a hypervisor can trigger the load-balancing mechanisms of the hypervisor to attempt to compensate for the load, resulting in mass resource strain.

Array-Based Replication

Array-based replication is a native function of storage array platforms which commonly operates without the need of additional datacenter resources. It tends to be highly efficient, as it transfers only data blocks that have changed, and not entire files. This efficiency usually results in little-to-no load being placed on the array's disk subsystem, ensuring high performance for applications and VMs during periods of replication. Since array-based replication occurs directly between storage array controllers, it reduces or removes any replication-based load on Guest VMs and hypervisor hosts.

Another benefit of this technology is that it is "software-agnostic," supporting both physical and virtual platforms. Array-based replication will preserve storage savings found on-disk, including data deduplication and compression, and will enhance these savings by compressing the data being sent between two arrays. Array-based replication can transfer snapshot backup data to other arrays, and in some cases, transfer data directly to tape.

Array-based replication is challenged to support heterogeneous array platforms, as array-based replication technologies are typically vendor-specific.

Disaster Recovery Automation

Data mobility delivered by virtual infrastructure platforms has enabled disaster recovery to be implemented through significantly simpler and more cost-effective means than what is possible with traditional physical servers. Prior to the advent of virtualization, disaster recovery was a menacing task: the capital expenditures associated with the deployment of identical datacenter resources (compute, network, and storage) in multiple sites immediately doubled the costs associated with applications requiring high availability.

From an operational standpoint, the situation was even worse. DR required significant investments in resources to create, verify, and regularly test the policies and procedures involved. These tests often had a negative impact on the production infrastructure, and as such administrators had to balance the need to test versus the need to maintain production: paradoxically, DR of a production environment could not be tested as the very testing itself disrupted production. This also caused great difficulties for architects and administrators who wished to make changes to production environments as it was extremely difficult to measure the impact of those changes on DR procedures.

The disaster recovery automation available within virtual infrastructures dramatically improves the performance and reliability of a DR environment. The resource abstraction of the hypervisor means assets required in each site do not have to be identical, thus providing cost savings. Virtualization also allows administrators to easily create recovery run-books within a matter of minutes.

Advanced storage array replication allows replicated datasets to be accessed via array cloning mechanisms, and thus testing of run-books can occur at any time without disrupting the production environment. This means production environments are freer to make changes and refinements as there is no down-stream impact on DR as would have been experienced in the past.

This tight integration of these automation applications, hypervisor management solutions, and array technologies dramatically decrease the amount of manual or administrator-driven tasks required for disaster recovery. This includes automatically mapping virtual machines to resources at the recovery site during a failover or test, and coordinating the boot up sequence of virtual machines in order to ensure infrastructure requirements are in place to support protected applications.

Both hypervisor and storage vendors provide DR automation tools. These range in capability, scope of supported platforms and price.

Note: Check if your replication solution will allow for tests to be completed in the recovery environment without interrupting production replication updates. If your solution requires you to stop replication in order to test, you may have great difficulty finding the time required to solve a DR issue without placing the production environment at risk.

Summary and Recommendations

There are many ways to back up and replicate data in a virtual infrastructure. We have provided a synopsis of the pros and cons of a number of technologies, and while we may struggle with suggesting an individual technology that is better than another, we don't suffer this challenge when we look at these technologies as they are applied in concert.

Historically, backup and disaster recovery are two separate processes, each requiring its own set of data, stored on a medium that has a single purpose. This model is a byproduct of the physical infrastructure. Cloud architects are pressed to restore services in the shortest period of time while also dramatically reducing the cost of day-to-day business continuance. Collapsing backup and DR seems like an ideal method to eliminate significant infrastructure overhead while achieving this form of agility.

The nature of copying data in a repetitive fashion on multiple forms of media, each with a single purpose introduces operational and capital inefficiencies that challenge the ability to deliver reasonable RTO. These use of technologies in their traditional manner, simply doesn't support cloud-computing initiatives.

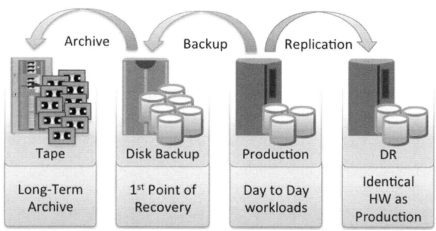

Figure 11-2: *An example of the redundant copy operations required with legacy backup & DR*

We recommend cloud architects implement the native DR capabilities of tier-1 applications and the needs of tier-2 applications are best met by unifying backup and DR processes into a single disk-based solution capable of providing the functions of both with fewer resource requirements.

Tier-1 applications have advanced to the point in which they provide the most robust and seamless set of backup and disaster recovery capabilities. Advanced array capabilities can accentuate the recovery points of these technologies.

Teir-2 applications, which are often the bulk of an organization's services, should be addressed in a unified manner. Snapshots can provide immediate, low-impact backups, which are stored on disk for a short-period of time. The on-disk nature ensures speedy recovery times. These backups can then be transferred to another set of disks, preferably offsite, and this disk can also service disaster recovery needs.

Clearly, the advancement of disk-based backups that preserve and transfer data in its native format can transform backup and remote replication for DR into a single, cost-effective, and unified process that meets the requirements of both from a more cost-effective and streamlined process.

Chapter 12
Datacenter Mobility & Enhanced Availability

Datacenter Mobility & Enhanced Availability

Cloud computing provides virtual infrastructures with the ability to non-disruptively migrate virtual machines and application workloads between hosts residing within and deployed across geographically distributed locations. This capability is commonly referred to as **datacenter mobility**, and contrary to popular belief, the desire for datacenter mobility is not the mobility itself, but rather the ability to ensure the survivability of an application and/or service in any eventuality.

In some regards, datacenter mobility is a new form of continuous availability for applications and non-disruptive datacenter operations for a number of use cases such as application resilience, consolidation and optimization of datacenter resources, and disaster avoidance.

In this chapter, we will review the technologies which enable these capabilities from the application layer through to the hypervisor, and how they extend to include enhanced networking and storage technologies. We will conclude with recommendations on deploying advanced applications and infrastructures purposely designed for multisite support, and that have no single point of failure.

Chapter Sections

The following sections will introduce you to the networking and storage constructs, including a comparison of the various types of storage required to span a virtual infrastructure between facilities and provide mobility for VMs:

Application Enabled Mobility
Discusses the capabilities of applications to span geographically distributed datacenters

Intra-Datacenter Mobility
Discusses the core concepts and requirements of datacenter mobility

Inter-Datacenter Mobility
Expands datacenter mobility across site boundaries with advanced networking, and the introduction of two forms of storage technologies: metro or stretched arrays and distributed storage caches

Replication with Disaster Recovery Automation
A brief look at applying DR mechanisms to solve intra-datacenter mobility challenges

Summary and Recommendations
Compares mobility options and prescribes a practical solution for enablement

Application Enabled Mobility

As discussed in the Backup and Disaster Recovery chapter, many of today's tier-1 applications include a deployment model that supports high availability with nodes distributed across geographically dispersed datacenters. Some of the more common applications to offer this functionality include Microsoft SQL Server and Exchange Server, and Oracle Database.

Application	High Availability Technology
Microsoft Exchange	Availability Groups
Microsoft SQL Server	Database Availability Groups
Oracle Database	Data Guard

Table 12-1: *Common high availability options that support geographic distribution*

All of the technologies listed above implement a form of log shipping between the virtual or physical nodes that represent the application cluster. Such a design provides a one-to-many replication model for advanced, multi-node configurations for the highest levels of availability. Log shipping requires a WAN connection capable of supporting the traffic generated by the application. By using the combination of online data in a remote location and the integration of the failover at the application layer, these tier-1 applications can provide non-disruptive services in the event of a single or multiple failures.

On the surface, high availability designs may not appear to be a means to provide datacenter mobility; however the ability to execute a controlled failover accomplishes this goal in the most graceful manner and with the least impact on end users. While one can obviously implement datacenter mobility with other means, those provided by the application are likely the best choice when considering the criticality of a tier-1 application.

Intra-Datacenter Mobility

The ability to non-disruptively migrate a virtual machine or a collection of VMs across servers and storage platforms with complete transaction integrity and no service interruption is critical in providing cloud computing services to consumers. Such technologies allow administrators the ability to perform proactive hardware migrations in order to balance workloads, simplify hardware refreshes, and free up valuable storage capacity in a datacenter.

To understand datacenter mobility, architects and administrators need to separate the ability to migrate individual VMs across CPU and memory resources (servers) from data (virtual disks) across storage objects. For those familiar with VMware, these capabilities are referred to as vMotion and Storage vMotion. A core requirement of this capability is that the physical hypervisor hosts share network resources, and the hypervisor must be configured for the non-disruptive migration of the compute resources. Similar requirements exist for non-disruptive migrations of virtual disks; the physical hypervisor hosts must have storage resources provided by a shared storage platform.

Advanced storage technologies exist which allow for the migration of datasets without the interaction of hypervisors or the virtual infrastructure operations. Technologies like storage profiles (discussed in Chapter 8, Virtual Storage Profiles) abstract the storage access from the hardware resources and can provide a means to migrate virtual disks, plus application and guest-connected storage LUNs and NAS file systems, between storage arrays and storage resources non-disruptively and en masse.

The combination of the more granular hypervisor enablements work well with the advanced array capabilities, as together they can accommodate individual virtual disks, non-encapsulated datasets, and mass migrations non-disruptively.

Inter-Datacenter Mobility

The ability to migrate a VM or collection of VMs between two datacenters is possible. It builds off of the foundation provided by hypervisors and through the advanced capabilities of networking and storage technologies. This capability is designed to provide the high availability that is found within tier-1 applications to all of the remaining applications in the datacenter.

At a basic level, Inter-Datacenter Mobility Requires hypervisor clusters, a Layer 2 Ethernet network, and shared storage access in both affected sites. Optionally, both sites may need a Fibre Channel network (see Chapter 3: SAN & NAS: Storage Protocols in the Cloud, for more details). These requirements mix physical and virtual infrastructure components, and have some restrictions and design consideration (including multiple storage options) to consider.

Note: These requirements change somewhat when expanding this capability beyond two datacenters. In the following discussions, we will focus on a 2-site deployment unless otherwise specified.

Datacenter mobility solutions will typically leverage existing non-disruptive migration technologies, like vMotion in VMware vSphere. To provide this capability over a distance longer than one finds in a datacenter requires a network link between the datacenters that provides communications with a **round trip latency of 5ms or less**. This latency value is often referred to as **round trip time (RTT)**. Contrary to common wisdom, geographical distance is only a limiting factor in mobility insofar as physical delays in data transmission violate this rigid latency requirement. In other words: cable length only matters if data can't travel it fast enough.

Spanning Layer 2 Networks

In order to receive the benefits of geographically dispersed datacenters, virtual machines migrations must be non-disruptive on the VM guest, or public, network. While IP addresses are layer 3 addresses, the larger challenge exists in ensuring optimal packet routing when spanning the layer 2 network.

Datacenter mobility requires one to extend the **Layer 2 (L2)** network between the remote datacenters. **LAN extensions** are required to ensure the communication between a VM and its connections are non-disruptive.

The use of LAN extensions presents a number of challenges, including maintaining site independence, transport independence, load balancing, path diversity, address scalability, etc. There are a number of established and emerging LAN extension technologies to consider, including **Multiprotocol Label Switching (MPLS)**, **Virtual Private Networking (VPN)**, **Overlay Transport Virtualization (OTV)**, and **Locator Identifier Separation Protocol (LISP)**.

Note: The authors highly recommend that you work with your networking vendor to receive the proper information and recommendations to ensure that your spanned network meets the requirements of your solution. This area of technology is advancing at a very rapid pace, and any specific recommendations would quickly become out of date.

Storage Capabilities Dictate Mobility Options

Currently, the storage industry primarily offers two forms of shared storage platform that provide datacenter mobility: **Metro & Stretched Clusters** and **Distributed Storage Caches**.

The more mature of the two offering is the geo-spanned storage cluster, also commonly referred to as a **stretched-cluster** or **metro-cluster**. The relatively newer option, distributed storage caches, is found in the market in architectures such as VPLEX from EMC, FlexCache from NetApp and Granite from Riverbed. Both technologies have their own strengths and shortcomings, as explained in the following sections.

Metro & Stretched Clusters

Enabling datacenter mobility via a metro or stretched cluster requires deployment of a VMware cluster and a highly available storage array configuration in which both hypervisor and storage controller nodes are located in separate datacenters. This design provides a similar set of functionality and capabilities to those found in traditional, single-datacenter deployments while providing datacenter mobility within a familiar framework.

The core storage functionality lies in the array's ability to write data synchronously to a local and remote **PLEX (aka set of disks)**. The controller at the remote site can promote the remote PLEX in order to support planned and unplanned events, such as datacenter maintenance, disaster avoidance, site or component failures, etc.

As metro or stretched arrays synchronously replicate data between two sites, they provide an immediate **"zero-copy" data migration** that is very beneficial should one need to quickly migrate a large quantity of VMs between two sites. With the storage already "migrated," one simply executes VM migrations from one site to the remote, and a mass "long distance vMotion" has been completed.

Note: Some storage vendors allow you to stripe datastores across multiple arrays. Before you deploy this architecture over a long distance, please ensure you understand the impact, both in terms of network bandwidth and time required to return the storage to normal operation and data protection.

Considerations with metro or stretched clusters
The primary challenges of the metro or stretched cluster solution are replication bandwidth requirements and the doubling of storage capacity requirements, both of which are required to support synchronous replication and data storage between the two sites. WAN acceleration technologies may be able to reduce some of the bandwidth requirements.

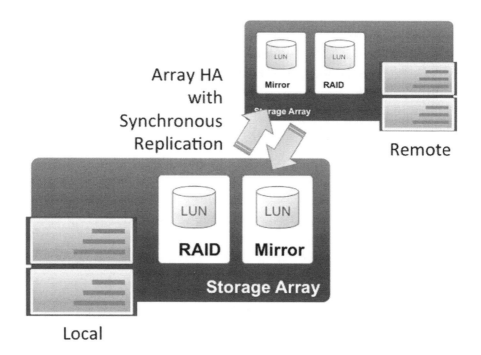

Figure 12-1: *An example of a metro or stretched storage array cluster*

Networking technologies may provide WAN acceleration services, or they may be provided natively by the storage array.

When considering the increase in storage capacity, an architect may view storage savings technologies like data deduplication or compression as a means to reduce the storage requirements. While these technologies will reduce storage consumption, they often cannot reduce the bandwidth requirements of the replication solution. As discussed in Chapter 5: Storage Saving Technologies, modern storage savings technologies often have trade-offs, such as running in real time or as a scheduled process.

While scheduled processes ensure the best performance for production workloads, they do not reduce the bandwidth required for replication as the storage savings are applied *after* the data has been written. By contrast, on-demand processes will reduce replication bandwidth, yet these technologies natively reduce overall storage performance, which is commonly observable with increased latencies. While some applications may be able to operate with these increased latencies, these increases will negatively impact the RTT, and as such, reduce the ability or distance over which one can synchronously replicate.

An ideal design eliminates the creation of redundant data while ensuring high performance and low latency. Some storage platforms provide hardware-based clones of virtual machines. This format differs significantly from the traditional method of provisioning a VM from a template, as the hardware clones only consume storage blocks that are unique to the datastore or storage array. This technology avoids the penalty of deploying VMs across wide-area uplinks.

Example: A 30GB VM clone may only require megabytes of data to be replicated with a hardware clone, whereas a traditional clone would require the full 30GB. Examples of this type of hardware accelerated VM clones are FlexClone from NetApp (for NFS & VMFS) and VNX from EMC (for NFS).

Distributed storage caches

Distributed storage caches provide a datacenter mobility architecture which is similar to a metro or stretch array from the perspective of the VMware technologies, although the storage architecture is very different. An architect must understand that a distributed storage cache requires all data access to be configured from the hypervisors to the cache that acts as a gateway or proxy for the actual array. Distributed caches are available in both hardware and software platforms.

A storage cache does not actually replicate the data between two sites but rather replicates the *metadata*, providing connected hosts with the appearance of a local copy of the remote data. This model enables the flexibility of per-VM migrations, which is a capability not natively inherent with a metro stretched array cluster.

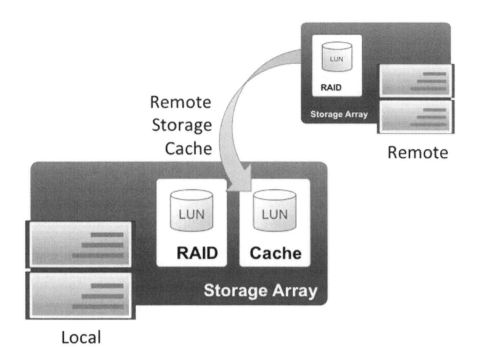

Figure 12-2: *An example of a distributed or remote storage cache*

Distributed caching technologies are available in both cache-specific hardware platforms or gateways and software-based capabilities running natively on storage arrays. Hardware-based gateway solutions may appear to provide caching capabilities similar to heterogeneous storage platforms; however, the caching capabilities are homogeneous, and the same caching capabilities must be deployed at all sites enabling datacenter mobility, whether it be via a hardware or a software based solution.

Considerations with distributed storage caches
The primary challenges of distributed storage cache architectures concern the time and network bandwidth required to complete migrations, and VM disruption due to network failures.

As the storage cache does not actually replicate the data between two sites, the data required to serve the I/O requests of VMs migrated through cache requires all of the VMs' data to be transferred on demand at the time the vMotion migration is executed. The increase in network bandwidth, and the time required to complete the transfer, are directly proportional to the number of VMs being simultaneously migrated.

As the cache enables VMs to run without having all of the data stored in the remote location, any disruption in the network will result in the disruption of all VMs being accessed from a remote cache.

Comparing Metro Stretched Array Clusters and Geo-Distributed Caches

Inter-datacenter mobility is a very attractive solution to provide agility to VMs and applications that natively lack a metro-stretched form of high-availability. The capabilities of the storage architecture will determine the aptness of the solution. The following table illustrates the some of these requirements, and how well they are met by the two solutions presented in this chapter.

	Metro Stretched Array Cluster	**Geo-Distributed Storage Cache**
Migration Level	Entire Array	Per VM
Daily Bandwidth Requirements	High	Low
Bandwidth Requirements at Time of Migration	Low	High
Migration Time requirements	Low	High

Table 12-2: *Comparison of requirements as pertinent to mobility between metro stretched clusters and distributed storage caches*

If you need to migrate individual VMs, then a distributed storage cache is likely the ideal platform for you. If your requirements include the ability to mass migrate a large number of VMs to address inter-datacenter maintenance or disaster avoidance initiatives, then a metro stretched array cluster is probably the best choice.

The ideal option would be to deploy a metro stretched array cluster that also provides a distributed storage caching mechanism. These types of architectures provide the best of both worlds: the ability to migrate individual VMs, and to execute on-demand mass migrations. Enabling software-based caching as a native function of your storage array will help you to avoid the acquisition and operational costs associated with deploying a distributed caching architecture.

Replication with Disaster Recovery Automation

Chapter 11 discussed disaster recovery in-depth, and we are revisiting this technology here as it does provide for a means of intra-datacenter mobility. While DR processes do not provide a non-disruptive means to enable services in a remote site, they do provide minimal disruption, and do not require the network and storage infrastructure upgrades, nor the distance limitation of the metro-spanned intra-datacenter mobility options. DR automation tools, like VMware Site Recovery Manager (SRM), handle the changes in infrastructure like IP address.

One needs to consider the costs of enabling intra-datacenter migrations with tier-2 applications. DR automation provides a cost effective and simple alternative if one can handle a 5-minute outage due to migration.

Summary and Recommendations

Datacenter mobility is an expansion of high availability that spans both local and remote datacenters. Like many solutions, there is no one-size-fits-all solution to maintain application uptime in the event of changes in workload demands, natural disasters, and infrastructure maintenance.

We recommend a two-technology approach to providing datacenter mobility. The first is to implement geo-spanned application high availability for the tier-1 applications. These designs best service the users of such mission/business critical applications. For all other applications, architects will need to evaluate and decide between the costs associated with, and downtime incurred when, one implements intra-datacenter versus automated disaster recovery technologies.

The second half of this approach isn't so clear. Intra-datacenter solutions built on metro-spanned storage clusters require high bandwidth WAN links, while a metro stretched storage array cluster doesn't. In both solutions, an architect must implement a spanned layer-2 network. By contrast, implementing array replication and DR automation is not non-disruptive, but the infrastructure costs are significantly less.

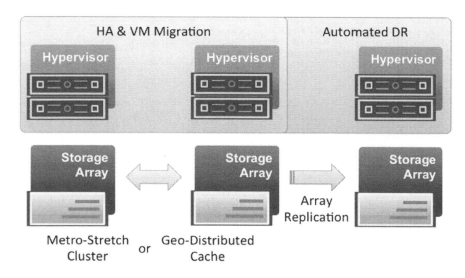

Figure 12-3: *An example of a metro stretched array cluster or geo-distributed cache with replication*

Chapter 13
Putting It All
Together: Storage
Optimized for the
Cloud

Putting It All Together: Storage Optimized for the Cloud

Until this chapter, we have reviewed each storage concept based on the merits each could provide in achieving the common goals of a shared, virtual infrastructure or cloud. While we stand behind our assessments and recommendations, a number of these technologies can negatively impact the ability of the others when deployed together.

In this chapter, we bring these technologies together. We will change our focus from individual components or capabilities over to whole solutions. The goal of this chapter is to help you to provision a shared storage infrastructure that includes the highest levels of availability, data protection, capacity utilization, and performance, while also remaining flexible in the face of unpredictable workloads.

It can be daunting to try to understand all of the options, capabilities, and limitations involved in designing architectures that will simultaneously provide a number of advanced storage technologies. Understanding where to best position these technologies in order to support your vSphere cloud could mean the difference between creating a robust, powerful, cutting-edge storage tool, or inestimable infrastructure failures for you and your organization.

Chapter Sections

This chapter includes the following sections to help you incorporate multiple cloud infrastructure technologies and techniques:

Common Goals of a Cloud Infrastructure
Reviews the goals of a cloud architect in deploying a successful storage infrastructure in support of a cloud architecture

Fiscal Responsibility
Discusses monetary considerations as the basis for all subsequent sections

Best-in-Class Availability
Recommendations regarding HA

Best-in-Class Data Protection
Recommendations regarding RAID

Best-in-Class Storage Savings
Recommendations for efficiencies

Best-in-Class Infrastructure Flexibility
Recommendations for flexibility

Best-in-Class Storage Performance
Recommendations regarding performance

Best-in-Class Backup & Disaster Recovery
Recommendations on restoring services and data

Conclusion

Brings all of the sections in this chapter together in a conclusive summary

Common Goals of a Cloud Infrastructure

In order to provide recommendations, we have to establish the core requirements for a shared storage platform in a virtualization environment. We want this design to be pragmatic, and to follow a 90/10 rule, in which 90% of all virtualized workloads run optimally and require little to no exceptions from the operational norm, with only 10% of workloads requiring special attention.

When designing shared infrastructures for cloud computing, the 90/10 rule is a valuable guideline for assessing technologies and their application within an architectural design. The rule allows an architect to focus on building systems that can support the vast majority of desired workloads without getting bogged down by fringe cases or strange exceptions. While no solution, no matter how sophisticated the technology, can address every single use case, the ability to build robust and flexible architectures minimizes the difficult exceptions an architect or administrator will have to handle.

Fiscal Responsibility

It is relatively easy to build a solution that is high-performing and highly-available, but is not fiscally responsible. A storage platform supporting a cloud infrastructure must be fiscally responsible while providing high availability, high performance and infrastructure flexibility.

The goal of any cloud infrastructure is to deliver cost-effective performance that is beyond that offered by traditional "silo" datacenters, but for any given organization, these performance metrics will differ. While one organization may prioritize data protection, another may value flexibility over any other concern, and a third organization may disregard both flexibility and data protection in favor of optimal storage performance and savings.

As such, the sections which follow seek to loosely define and explain the parameters you will use to evaluate a storage solution before concluding with the author's recommendations.

Best-in-Class Availability

This requirement may seem basic and obvious, but it needs to be stated: no network architect should ever consider deploying a non-High-Availability storage controller platform in a production cloud deployment - the impact of a storage layer failure will certainly result in downtime, and could also result in permanent data loss, this is not a place to shortchange the infrastructure.

Best-in-Class Data Protection

RAID technologies for physical servers were designed to provide either minimal data protection at a low cost or extensive data protection at a high cost. None of these traditional RAID technologies are suitable for delivering a high-performance, highly available, and cost-effective storage infrastructure.

The infrastructures supporting cloud computing initiatives are extremely dense, and they must be able to survive the simultaneous failure of more than a single disk drive. As such, the ideal data protection formats appear to be RAID 6 and NetApp's proprietary RAID-DP. Both of these data protection technologies ensure data availability in the event of multiple physical drive failures, and can provide this protection with minimal cost overhead.

A RAID 6 storage array must include some form of advanced storage caching or tiering (comprised of solid-state media) in order to address the RAID calculations associated with the workload demands of most production data sets. This form of RAID 6 is significantly more cost-effective than any RAID 10 solution, and requires less rack space and power to operate.

We include NetApp's RAID-DP in our recommendation as it is the likely the most widely deployed propriety RAID format in the market today. RAID-DP matches RAID 6 in delivering high data protection levels with very low storage capacity overhead. RAID-DP excels in RAID computations and disk writes. These advantages lessen the need for advanced storage caching or tiering to achieve high performance.

Best-in-Class Storage Savings

As data grows, and cost pressures mount, it is not a question of *if* you will be required to enable storage saving capabilities throughout all tiers and use cases within your infrastructure, but a question of *when*. To enable these capabilities, a storage platform must provide either block-level data deduplication or inline data compression. Ideally, a system would provide both for use with any storage protocol.

Block-Level Data Deduplication

Block level data deduplication reduces the storage capacity required to store multiple data objects without modifying the native format of data. It allows for the sharing of globally unique binary blocks of data to be referenced by multiple data objects, such as virtual machines, databases, and unstructured files. The result is that this technology enables each data object, such as a virtual machine, to only consume unique data blocks on the storage array.

Contrary to common knowledge, the sharing of binary blocks of data in multiple data objects can actually improve overall system performance. By increasing the number of read requests that can be resolved by system cache, block sharing can lead to a reduction in overall seek times required by the disk subsystem in order to meet I/O requests from two different virtual machines (or data objects).

Block-level data de-duplication should be considered a storage industry standard requirement, and used with every dataset hosting a VMware vSphere virtual or cloud infrastructure.

Data Compression

Another valuable storage saving technology is data compression. While similar to data de-duplication, data compression provides a method for reducing storage requirements of datasets that do not share common blocks between one another. Instead, data compression uses space-saving algorithms to reduce the physical footprint of a data set.

Data compression should be considered a required capability on any storage array when deploying a VMware vSphere virtual or cloud infrastructure. It is the only means to reduce the storage requirements with a number of use cases, including encrypted data and data stored in objects like messaging platform databases.

Best-in-Class Infrastructure Flexibility

Between SAN and NAS, there is no significant difference between the performance and capabilities of the SAN protocols (Fibre Channel, Fibre Channel over Ethernet, iSCSI), and the NAS protocols (Network File System (NFS) and Server Message Block (SMB)) in terms of data throughput, obtainable IOPS, array and guest CPU utilization, and latency.

Storage protocol flexibility is more important than most architects realize - the hardware deployed to support a solution today may remain in place and unchanged for years; however, today more than ever, the market is experiencing a rate of technological innovation that is outpacing current rates of asset depreciation. Hypervisor vendors are cycling their major software releases every 24 months, while many hardware depreciation schedules range from 36 to 60 months. Selecting a storage architecture that is inflexible commits an architect to a protocol or software that may become obsolete at the mid-life point of coexisting physical assets.

Storage platform flexibility helps an architect to avoid taking on technological debt: We recommend that architects consider investing in flexible infrastructure within the interconnect, fabric, and storage platform.

Best-in-Class Storage Performance

We have reviewed performance characteristics of various media types, including rotating and solid-state disk drives, as well as enhanced storage caching mechanisms in both the host and on the storage array. The authors of this book are not confident that the next several years will provide high capacity, highly resilient, low-cost solid-state disk drives. As such we support hybrid solutions that leverage advanced storage caching mechanisms.

Structured and Unstructured Data

Many storage platforms are designed to specifically service either structured or unstructured data. Problematically, these boutique-style arrays lack the ability to service the unexpected workloads that a cloud consumer may choose to deploy. Purchasing separate arrays for different types of data access should be avoided whenever possible. An architect should verify that the storage platform he or she is considering can support performance-oriented databases just as well as it can serve workgroups or home directories.

Advanced Storage Array Caching

The ideal storage media for shared infrastructure should provide large storage capacity at a relatively low price while also being able to automatically respond to unexpected changes in I/O demands from the application layer.

Storing data on inexpensive rotating media that can respond to increases in workload with solid-state media caches (in the form of DRAM or SSD) is an ideal means of providing responsiveness to an array platform. Most of these caches are modular in nature, and can be non-disruptively added to production arrays.

For example, NetApp's array platform leverages block sharing in data deduplication, pointer based cloning, and snapshots. NetApp has extended this capability to their storage array cache, which in effect provides greater performance by reducing the calls to the disk subsystem while also increasing the amount of addressable capacity in the storage cache. This model maps to what VMware provides with transparent page sharing in the hypervisor, and seems to be appropriate for use in a cloud.

Host-Side Caching

When running performance-sensitive applications, consider deploying host-based cache expansion technologies like Fusion-IO and the WarpDrive from LSI. These host-side caches are comprised of PCI-based NAND Flash, which is designed to extend the performance capability of a storage array cache into the host. This technology is becoming a reasonable way to extend the performance capability of a storage array without upgrading the system hardware, and is particularly valuable with performance-dense workloads such as databases.

Storage Tiering

As storage tiering requires additional I/O to migrate data between various types of storage media, it is not an ideal means of dynamically responding to increases in workload. The migration process will actually exacerbate the load on the array, resulting in even greater performance issues.

Storage tiering, whether automatic or manual, is tremendously valuable as a means to non-disruptively demote storage to a lower cost tier. In this use case, storage tiering focuses on inactive data, and moves it to the storage medium best suited to the data's long-term archiving and retention. Storage caching mechanisms ensure that, should this data be called in the future, it will be served from a high-performing solid-state cache.

Best-in-Class Backup & Disaster Recovery

Backup and disaster recovery are unfortunately the price of admission when one hosts a production environment. Today datacenters copy data ad nauseum in order to ensure production, backup, and disaster recovery needs are met.

We recommend cloud architects implement the native DR capabilities of tier-1 applications and the needs of tier-2 applications are best met by unifying backup and DR processes into a single disk-based solution capable of providing the functions of both with fewer resource requirements.

The nature of copying data in a repetitive fashion on multiple forms of media, each with a single purpose introduces operational and capital inefficiencies that challenge the ability to deliver reasonable RTO. These use of technologies in their traditional manner, simply doesn't support cloud-computing initiatives.

Conclusion

The recommendations presented above can be implemented either in tandem with, or wholly independent of, each other. Architects focusing on building a cloud may be looking for storage attributes in the form of resource pools and rapid elasticity. These may be terms with which a storage admin is unfamiliar. Either way, the goal for any datacenter architect is to develop an agile, high-performance, highly available, and fiscally responsible storage platform for use in a cloud deployment. Taking the above recommendations individually can help you to meet your organization's stated goals, but incorporating a multi-faceted architectural approach will create a datacenter that is greater than the sum of its parts.

We have a very basic rule to manage this complex topic. Seek technologies that align to the 90/10 rule: no matter how many "best practices" one implements, they rarely will attain 100% workload optimization. 90%, while still a high percentage, is a realistic figure in a carefully planned and implemented cloud strategy. The 10% represents the outliers, the edge cases. 10% is management by exception, which in turn is easy to manage.

Finally: remember that virtualization changes everything. With careful research, proper planning, and patient deployment, you can be sure that for your datacenter, virtualization will be a change for the better!

References

Blacharski, D. (2009) How much can your vendor increase your storage utilization? *Data Protection 360*. Retrieved from http://www.itworld.com/storage/69788/how-much-can-your-vendor-increase-your-storage-utilization

Chen, G., Woo, B. & Yezhkova, N (2011). Worldwide Storage and Virtualized x86 Environments 2011 - 2015 Forecast. *IDC.com*. Doc #231080. Retrieved from http://www.idc.com/getdoc.jsp?containerId=231080

Crump, G. (2010). Increasing Storage Utilization Rates. *Informationweek.com*. Retrieved from http://www.informationweek.com/news/storage/data_protection/2292029 10

Direct NFS. n.d. Retrieved 16 March 2012 from the Orafaq wiki. http://www.orafaq.com/wiki/Direct_NFS

Hodak, W. & Closson, K. (2007). Oracle Database 11g Direct NFS Client. *Oracle.com*. Retrieved from http://www.oracle.com/technetwork/articles/directnfsclient-11gr1-twp-129785.pdf

Jafr, S. & Lemmons, C. (2011). Storage Performance: Measuring FCoE, FC, iSCSI, and NFS Protocols. *NetApp.com*. Paper # TR-3916. Retrieved from http://www.netapp.com/templates/mediaView?m=tr-3916.pdf&cc=us&wid=121692284&mid=50324994

Merean, L. (2010). Wasted Space: IT Aims to Fill Disks. *Computerworld.com*. Retrieved from http://www.computerworld.com/s/article/351035/Wasted_Space_IT_Aims_to_Fill_Disks

Oracle Storage Guy, The. (31 March 2009) "New DNS Performance Results" Retrieved 2 February 2012 from http://oraclestorageguy.typepad.com/oraclestorageguy/2009/03/new-dnfs-performance-results.html

Slisinger, M. & Stewart, V. (2006). Network Appliance and VMware ESX Server 2.5.x: Building a Virtual Infrastructure from Server to Storage. *dnscoinc.com*. Paper # TR-3482. Retrieved from http://www.dnscoinc.com/wp_netapp_8.pdf

Glossary of Terms

AFR

Annualized Failure Rate. The expected failure rate during a year of a given set of components, expressed as a percentage. This is calculated using the Mean Time Between Failure (MTBF) of the components and the number of hours they will be expected to run during the year (Typically 8,760 hours for components that run 24/7).

ALUA

Asymmetric Logical Unit Access. A multipathing standard that allows hosts and arrays to seamlessly negotiate path management policies (such as preferred vs. non-preferred paths).

CIFS

Common Internet File System. See SMB below.

BER

Bit Error Rate or Bit Error Ratio. The expected amount of bits that will be inadvertently altered during transmission or storage due to medium or communication errors.

CNA

Converged Network Adapter. A host device that combines the functionality of a Host Bus Adapter (HBA) and a Network Interface Controller (NIC). Provides storage and network connectivity through the same device.

DAS

Direct-attached Storage. A storage term that generally refers to storage devices directly attached to a server or host, without a storage network or between. Used to differentiate from storage devices that use SAN or NAS.

Deduplication

A technology that involves identifying duplicate data in a dataset and discarding the redundant data without changing the logical structure of the data. Used to reduce storage consumption of a dataset and therefore the cost of storing it. Commonly implemented at either the file level (removing duplicate files) or block level (removing duplicate blocks).

eMLC

Enterprise Multi Level Cell. In the storage industry, used to designate solid state and flash memory technology with low error rates that make them appropriate for use in enterprise grade primary storage solutions.

FC

Fibre Channel. A networking technology primarily used for storage networking.

FCP

Fibre Channel Protocol. A SAN transport protocol used for transporting SCSI commands over Fibre Channel networks.

FCoE (SAN)

Fibre Channel over Ethernet. A SAN technology that transports Fibre Channel frames over an Ethernet network.

File Share

Common term for a shared NAS volume, typically used for storing application or user data over a network to a storage array.

GCS (Guest Connected Storage)
A storage architecture option that involves connecting a virtual machine guest directly to a SAN or NAS storage object, without using the storage management layer of the hypervisor. This is typically done for the purposes of ensuring high performance or meeting application specific storage requirements.

HBA
Host Bus Adapter. A host device that is used to connect to storage devices over a storage network.

High Availability (HA)
Either refers to the solution design concept of building systems that provide the maximum possible uptime to applications and services, or to the technologies which enable and ensure this uptime. Will usually be divided into tiers defined by uptime metrics delivered, cost, and complexity.

Host-Side Caching
A relatively new caching technology that uses solid state or DRAM based expansion modules and cache management software in hosts to improve storage performance.

Hypervisor
A hardware virtualization technology that allow multiple virtual machines, or guests, to run on the same physical host server.

I/O
Input/Ouput. In the storage industry, generally refers to data communication between a host and storage devices or arrays.

IDC

International Data Corporation. A market research and analysis firm focusing on information technology, among other areas.

iSCSI

Internet Small Computer System Interface. A SAN technology designed for carrying SCSI commands over IP networks.

LUN

Logical Unit Number. A storage device accessed by SAN protocols such as FCP, iSCSI and FCoE.

MSCS

Microsoft Cluster Server. A service that allows multiple Microsoft Windows Servers to work together in a cluster. Primarily used to ensure application or service reliability in the event of physical device failures.

NAS

Network-attached Storage. A storage device providing file level storage services over a Ethernet network. Typically used as a file server for user and application data.

NFS

Network File System. A distributed file system protocol designed to allow hosts to access files from a remote storage device over a network.

NIC

Network Interface Controller. Commonly known as a network adapter or Ethernet adapter. A host device used for connection to a network.

RDM

Raw Device Mapping. The name within VMware vSphere for a pass-thru LUN, a LUN connected from a storage array directly to a Virtual Machine's Guest Operating System, with the hypervisor only serving as a physical proxy.

SAN

Storage Area Network. A network dedicated to providing access to block level storage devices.

SAS

Serial Attached SCSI. A communication protocol used to move data between hosts and storage devices. In the storage industry, also commonly used to designate high performance drives with SAS interfaces.

SATA

Serial ATA / Serial AT Attachment. A communication protocol used to move data between hosts and storage devices. In the storage industry, also commonly used to designate high capacity, lower performance drives with SATA interfaces.

Share

See File Share.

SIOC

Storage I/O Control. A capability of VMware vSphere which allows administrators to create policies that ensure proportional fairness when multiple virtual machines access a shared storage resource.

SMB

Server Message Block. A network file sharing protocol formerly known as CIFS. Typically used by Microsoft Windows Hosts.

SMB over RDMA

SMB over Remote Direct Memory Access. An accelerated storage connectivity protocol which works by allowing applications to bypass most of the software and operating system layers and communicate directly to hardware.

SSD

Solid-state Drive (or Disk). A disk technology comprised of non-mechanical media, typically NAND-based flash memory.

(SDRS) Storage DRS

Storage Dynamic Resource Scheduler. A VMware storage management feature that creates a pool of datastores (called a Datastore Cluster) and then automatically manages the location of virtual machine storage objects within that pool. This may include automatically moving objects for the purpose of ensuring proper storage performance.

Storage Tiering

A data management concept that involves locating different datasets (or portions of a dataset) on storage pools with different capabilities including disk media type, cache state and data protection level based on the performance requirements of the dataset.

VAAI

vSphere API Array Integration. A set of VMware APIs that allows the vSphere hypervisor to interact directly with a storage array for the purpose of improving and optimizing common operations (such as I/O offloading, array based cloning etc.)

VADP

vStorage APIs for Data Protection. A set of VMware APIs that allow backup software to protect virtual machines across multiple VMware hosts from a centralized backup server without requiring agents in each virtual machine or vSphere host.

VLAN – Virtual LAN or Virtual Local Area Network. Used to group devices on a network independent of the physical network configuration. Accomplished by "tagging" hosts and interfaces with a VLAN ID.

VMFS – VMware Virtual Machine File System. A clustered file system used by VMware to allow multiple hosts and virtual machine guests to simultaneously access a shared SAN storage device.

VSA – Virtual Storage Appliance (or Array). A storage solution that uses storage management software in a virtual machine guest, rather than dedicated hardware. This enables the use of some advanced storage capabilities in environments where the dedicated hardware would be inappropriate.

WWN – World Wide Name. A unique host or port identifier used with storage networking such as Fibre Channel.